A BRAVE NEW SERIES

GLOBAL ISSUES IN A CHANGING WORLD

This new series of short, accessible think-pieces deals with leading global issues of relevance to humanity today. Intended for the enquiring reader and social activists in the North and the South, as well as students, the books explain what is at stake and question conventional ideas and policies. Drawn from many different parts of the world, the series' authors pay particular attention to the needs and interests of ordinary people, whether living in the rich industrial or the developing countries. They all share a common objective – to help stimulate new thinking and social action in the opening years of the new century.

Global Issues in a Changing World is a joint initiative by Zed Books in collaboration with a number of partner publishers and non-governmental organizations around the world. By working together, we intend to maximize the relevance and availability of the books published in the series.

PARTICIPATING NGOS

Both ENDS, Amsterdam
Catholic Institute for International Relations, London
Corner House, Sturminster Newton
Council on International and Public Affairs, New York
Dag Hammarskjöld Foundation, Uppsala
Development GAP, Washington DC
Focus on the Global South, Bangkok
Inter Pares, Ottawa
Public Interest Research Centre, Delhi
Third World Network, Penang
Third World Network–Africa, Accra
World Development Movement, London

About this Series

'Communities in the South are facing great difficulties in coping with global trends. I hope this brave new series will throw much needed light on the issues ahead and help us choose the right options.'

MARTIN KHOR, *Director,*
Third World Network, Penang

'There is no more important campaign than our struggle to bring the global economy under democratic control. But the issues are fearsomely complex. This Global Issues series is a valuable resource for the committed campaigner and the educated citizen.'

BARRY COATES, *Director,*
World Development Movement (WDM)

'Zed Books has long provided an inspiring list about the issues that touch and change people's lives. The Global Issues series is another dimension of Zed's fine record, allowing access to a range of subjects and authors that, to my knowledge, very few publishers have tried. I strongly recommend these new, powerful titles and this exciting series.'

JOHN PILGER, *author*

'We are all part of a generation that actually has the means to eliminate extreme poverty world-wide. Our task is to harness the forces of globalization for the benefit of working people, their families and their communities – that is our collective duty. The Global Issues series makes a powerful contribution to the global campaign for justice, sustainable and equitable development, and peaceful progress.'

GLENYS KINNOCK, MEP

ABOUT THE AUTHOR

JOHN MADELEY has been a writer and broadcaster specialising in Third World development and environmental issues for the past twenty years. From 1983 to 1998 he was editor of the renowned magazine *International Agricultural Development*. A contributor to leading British papers including the *Observer*, *Guardian*, and *Financial Times*, he has also written for many voluntary organizations including Christian Aid, CAFOD, the Catholic Institute for International Relations, the Panos Institute, and the Swedish-based Forum Syd. He is the author of several books: *When Aid is No Help: How Projects Fail and How They Could Succeed*; *Trade and the Poor: The Impact of International Trade on Developing Countries*; *Land is Life: Land Reform and Sustainable Agriculture* (co-editor); *Big Business, Poor Peoples: The Impact of Transnational Corporations on the World's Poor*; and *Hungry for Trade: How the Poor Pay for Free Trade*.

CRITICAL ACCLAIM FOR THIS BOOK

'I welcome John Madeley's new book as another contribution to the debate on world hunger and the role of agriculture. His long experience in this field has enabled him to draw together many strands in this synoptic volume and I hope that it will help stimulate decision-makers to muster the necessary political will and resources to tackle the scourges of hunger and undernutrition that still affect more than eight hundred million people worldwide. With the prospect of continued growth in the world's population in the coming decades, the role of agriculture is pivotal to the final eradication of hunger.'

JACQUES DIOUF, Director-General of the Food and Agriculture Organization of the United Nations (FAO)

'A timely book illustrating how a great range of technologies and processes are promoting transitions towards agricultural sustainability that are in turn improving both environments and the lives of the poor.'

PROFESSOR JULES PRETTY,
University of Essex

'John Madeley unmasks the global effort to deprive the South of its ability to feed itself, to shift the focus from self-reliance to complete dependence, and to move from sustainable farming practices to environment-unfriendly industrial agricultural systems.'

DEVINDER SHARMA, food and trade
policy analyst, New Delhi

FOOD FOR ALL

The Need for a New Agriculture

JOHN MADELEY

UNIVERSITY PRESS LTD
Dhaka

DAVID PHILIP
Cape Town

FERNWOOD PUBLISHING LTD
Halifax, Nova Scotia

BOOKS FOR CHANGE
Bangalore

WHITE LOTUS CO. LTD
Bangkok

ZED BOOKS
London & New York

To Alison with love, forty years on

Food for All
was first published in 2002 by

Bangladesh: The University Press Ltd, Red Crescent Building,
114 Motijheel C/A, PO Box 2611, Dhaka 1000

Burma, Cambodia, Laos, Thailand and Vietnam: White Lotus Co. Ltd,
GPO Box 1141, Bangkok 10501, Thailand

Canada: Fernwood Publishing Ltd, PO Box 9409 Station A,
Halifax, Nova Scotia, Canada B3K 5S3

India: Books for Change, 139 Richmond Road, Bangalore 560 025, India

Southern Africa: David Philip Publishers (Pty Ltd), 208 Werdmuller Centre,
Claremont 7735, South Africa

Rest of the world:
Zed Books Ltd, 7 Cynthia Street, London N1 9JF, UK,
and Room 400, 175 Fifth Avenue, New York, NY 10010, USA

Distributed in the USA exclusively by Palgrave, a division of
St Martin's Press, LLC, 175 Fifth Avenue, New York, NY 10010, USA

Designed and typeset in Monotype Bembo by Illuminati, Grosmont
Cover designed by Andrew Corbett.
Printed and bound in the United Kingdom by Cox & Wyman, Reading

A catalogue record for this book is available from the British Library

Library of Congress Cataloging-in-Publication Data applied for

ISBN 1 84277 018 7 (Hb)
ISBN 1 84277 019 5 (Pb)

Canada ISBN 1 55266 083 4
South Africa ISBN 0 86486 590 2
India ISBN 81 87380 67 5

Contents

1 INTRODUCTION   1
   Food 3
   The Issues 5
   War on Hunger? 8

2 HISTORICAL PERSPECTIVES   10
   'Total Change' 12
   The Problem with Western-Style Agriculture 14
   BSE: Trigger for Change 16
   Learning from Whom? 18

3 THIRD WORLD AGRICULTURE:
   WHO GROWS WHAT?   20
   Crops for Food 21
   Crops for Export 23
   The Methods: Intercropping versus Monocropping 26
   Wisdom, Not Chemicals 30

4 THE HUNGRY   32
   Who Are the Hungry? 33
   The International Commitment 34
   Since the World Food Summit 36
   And Now? 39

5   THE NEW AGRICULTURE   41

Sustainable Agriculture   42
Permaculture   43
Evidence from Africa, Asia and Latin America   44

6   GETTING THE TECHNOLOGIES RIGHT   52

The International Agricultural Research Centres   52
GM Technology   59

7   THE WATER SPRING   66

How Much Is There?   66
Irrigation: Big Dams and Little Dams   67
Harvesting Water   71
Putting Floods to Use   73
Drainage is Vital   74
Making Water Go Further   76
Digging Deeper – A Solution?   78
Productivity and Pricing   78

8   WHEN LAND IS LIFE   81

Land Tenure: An Issue that Won't Go Away   81
Slow Progress   84
The World Bank Under Fire   85

9   WOMEN FOOD PRODUCERS:
RELEASING THEIR POTENTIAL   91

Gender Bias – Despite Women's Increasing Role   92
What Needs to Change?   94

10   THE CREDIT LINE   100

Microcredit: How it Works   101
Questionable Credit   104
The Challenge   106

11   RURAL DEVELOPMENT:
THE WIDER CONTEXT   107

The Services Needed   108
New Sources of Energy   111
Access to Markets   112

12   THE ROLE OF TRADE   115

       The WTO Agreement on Agriculture's Impact on the
            Poor   118
       How Transnational Corporations Dominate
            Agriculture   121
       Food versus Export Crops: The Right Balance   126

13   ENVIRONMENTAL IMPACTS   129

       Global Warming: The Indisputable Dangers   129
       Soil: The Cradle of Production   134
       Desertification: Another Threat   138
       Monoculture: Why so Dangerous?   139
       Deforestation   140

14   LIVESTOCK CONNECTIONS   143

       Animal Traction   145
       Animal Species in Decline   146
       The Meat Problem   147
       Overfishing   149

15   OFFICIAL AGENCIES   153

       World Bank: The Record   153
       United Nations Agencies   157

16   CONCLUSION: AGRICULTURE MATTERS   160

       Why Prioritise Agriculture?   160
       Aid that Works   162
       An Economic Environment that Does Not
            Hinder   163
       A New Direction   165

     NOTES   167

     FURTHER READING   178

     RELEVANT ORGANISATIONS
     INCLUDING WEBSITES   180

List of Boxes and Tables

Boxes

Agricultural Poverty   39

How Crops for Export Can Be Grown Organically:
   The Case of Ethiopian Coffee   51

International Agricultural Research Centres   58

Appropriate Research   59

GM 'Will Not Feed the Hungry'   65

Promoting Farmer Involvement in Irrigation   79

Land Loss   88

Land Reform in the Philippines   89

Gender and Genetic Engineering   98

Women Farmers and Legumes in Zambia   98

Educational Fees and Food Security   114

No Food Security without Soil Security   136

Tables

World Food Production and Trade, 1968–1998   116

Patent Holders on Six Leading Staple Foods   125

CHAPTER I

INTRODUCTION

*We have within our grasp the ability to feed the world
and conserve its irreplaceable resources*

Miguel Altieri

Around 10,000 years ago a woman from a plant-gathering tribe
returned home after a long day collecting seed in the wild. She
stumbled, and the basket with the collected seed fell to the ground.
The woman picked up the seed as best she could but some remained
on the soil and eventually became buried. The rains came, spring
and winter passed and when the woman was collecting food the
following summer, she happened to pass the place where she had
dropped the seed the previous autumn. To her surprise she noticed
grain growing in abundance on the spot. She scattered more seed on
the ground that year and to her delight it once again yielded results.
This happened somewhere on the Middle East's fertile crescent – the
arc that extends from Palestine through Syria, southern Turkey, Iraq
and western Iran – and marked the start of planting and harvesting
seeds for food, of the state of agriculture itself.[1]

What happened when that woman stumbled with her seed was
the beginning of a new chapter in human development. For the
plant-gatherers it meant more food. Today, 10,000 years later, another
chapter needs opening for the millions of people who are chronically
short of food. This requires:

- *A new approach to agriculture* that breaks out of a pattern of farming that leaves too many in hunger.
- *New policies from governments* that learn from farmers, new thinking, new structures, new institutions.
- *New ways of releasing women's contribution* to food production – a contribution often overlooked and ignored by policymakers.
- *A new synthesis of farming practices* for millions of small-scale farmers that recover and combine traditional ways with recent and innovative technologies.

All this can be done – helped by the Internet, which means that knowledge can be imported instantly from anywhere in the world within hours. Central to the approach of this book is the conviction that there is a pattern of agriculture and a wider economic order that can and will provide food for all.

The book looks at the type of agriculture needed for everyone to have adequate food as quickly as possible in the twenty-first century, and to meet the pledge made by world leaders at the 1996 World Food Summit to halve the number of food-insecure people by 2015 'as a first step' to ensuring food for all. As Chapter 4 makes clear, the declaration of leaders made at that summit is welcome, if limited. For in a world of unprecedented wealth the amount of hunger is a scandal that needs ending, not halving. Agricultural systems are needed that can feed the world within years rather than decades. But the 2015 target is at least a marker.

This book focuses chiefly on resource-poor farmers, because it is they who are among those suffering most from hunger, and it is from them that increases in food output can and must come. Many of the technologies that are needed today have been used by farmers for centuries. But often they need to be renewed. Some of the techniques are in danger of being lost to the point that when they are rediscovered they are seen as 'new'. In May 2001, for example, the World Bank website contained details of a new report: 'Common Ground, Common Future: How Eco-agriculture Can Help Feed the World and Save Wild Biodiversity', published by the World Conservation Union and Future Harvest. The Bank's website says that the report 'outlines a new solution to the biodiversity extinction, called "eco-agriculture", which seeks to help farmers, most urgently those living in or near biodiversity hotspots, to grow more food while conserving habitats critical to wildlife'. The approach 'dramatically breaks with both traditional conservation policies and common agriculture techniques'.[2]

But eco-agriculture has a far larger role in feeding the world than 'conserving habitats critical to wildlife'. The fact that the World Bank presents eco-agriculture as a 'new solution' speaks volumes, for this type of agriculture has been practised by millions of resource-poor farmers for centuries. It is the World Bank and other official agencies that have promoted 'common agriculture techniques', more specifically chemically intensive 'modern agriculture', and have done their best to push eco-agriculture aside. But there is joy in heaven over one sinner who repents!

Another aspect of 'newness' is the way that citizens' groups all over the world are making it clear that the old ways of doing things are not good enough, that too many people are being left out, that any system that does not feed everyone is wrong. Many feel that the political process is not responding quickly enough to the urgency of the situation. Many thousands have taken to the streets of Seattle, Prague, Washington, Genoa and other cities, highlighting not just a new idealism but a demand for a new order where profits are not as important as vulnerable people. 'People clearly feel it is time to emphasise values and not just talk monetarily about adding value. There is a change of spirit as well as a change of pace'.[3]

FOOD

Food is more than a commodity that is sold and bought. It is more than the nutrients we consume. Food is a unique and bonding resource that should be shared at every level: family, community, national and international. Yet almost 800 million people are estimated to be chronically short of food. And for around 2,000 million others, living on the equivalent of less than two dollars a day, food shortages are common.

The imperative of every man, woman and child having enough food to eat is a sentiment that unites people throughout the world.

It is a deeply held religious, humanitarian and moral concern that is stressed in all the world's major religions. 'Give us today our daily bread' is part of the prayer that is central to the Christian faith. The urgency, the immediacy of the need for bread is seen by the use of the word 'today'. Giving alms to the poor and fasting in Ramadan are central to Islam. The alleviation of suffering is a vital precept of Buddhism. In the Sikh religion, feeding people is seen as a religious duty. And it was a Hindu, Mahatma Gandhi, who reminded the world that 'a starving man sees God only in a loaf of bread'.

Bertolt Brecht's *The Threepenny Opera* reminds us that morality and food run together: 'First we eat then comes morality'. Can these widely held beliefs and feelings be translated into ensuring that a hungry world is transformed into a well-fed world?

Some of the reasons why people lack food lie outside agriculture. People go hungry because they are too poor either to grow enough or to buy the food they need. Growing more food may not in itself reduce poverty. Overcoming poverty requires a many-sided strategy, from education to rural development. But agriculture is the economic base of most of the poor and hungry.

The right kind of agriculture can make an important contribution to poverty alleviation, food security and economic growth and development. Agriculture yields benefits that extend beyond food production, for example in employment and the development of rural communities. An increase in agricultural productivity can be the trigger for growth and poverty reduction. 'Reviving agriculture is not the whole of the answer to rural poverty although it is a big part of it'.[4]

Again the challenge is not just to produce more food. The world already produces enough food, overall. This is one reason why genetic modification technology, with its promise of increased food output, does not address the real issues. The challenge is for the food to be produced *by* the people who need it most, *for* the people who need it most. The challenge is to produce food on small-scale farms and to create the conditions that enable people who suffer from chronic hunger to have the food they need for a healthy life.

THE ISSUES

This book begins with a historical perspective, looking at the way agriculture has developed down the centuries. It goes on to review the crisis that affects Western agriculture, at the way agriculture has been industrialised and has forced tens of thousands of farmers off the land. Western-style, chemical-based agriculture is now facing a host of problems. Soils are being undermined by chemicals, making it difficult to sustain yields, pests are becoming resistant and diversity is being lost, narrowing the base on which food production depends. Loss of biodiversity, soil erosion and desertification have reduced the productive capacity of agricultural land. Western agriculture, concludes Chapter 2, has no moral right to be considered a model for Third World countries to follow.

Chapter 3 considers the crops for food and for export that are grown in developing countries today, and the methods that are used. Intercropping, it notes, has a long and successful history, with resource-poor farmers down the ages evolving the systems to produce the food they needed. Chemical-style agriculture, introduced in the twentieth century, has both failed and misled the poor. Many resource-poor farmers were persuaded that the answer to their problems lay in a packet, in a can of chemicals, such as fertilisers and pesticides. They abandoned traditional techniques in favour of methods that promised higher yields and improved incomes. Monocropping has taken sections of Third World agriculture down a wrong path, concludes the chapter, but many farmers are now recovering and developing traditional techniques once again.

Who are the hungry? asks Chapter 4. It looks at the international commitment to halving their number by 2015 and at the progress since that commitment was given. Progress has been too slow; the hungry are still being let down by the lack of priority given to their plight by policymakers. Many governments still do not have the policies to match their commitments.

There is hope and it lies with people and their inventiveness. Chapter 5 is a chapter of hope, examining some of the ways in which farmers are increasing their output of food. How small farmers in Madagascar, for example, have developed a new way of growing rice that yields substantially more; how farmers in Nepal are successfully using permaculture techniques to raise output; how farmers in Brazil and Ecuador are increasing output. Exciting developments are happening all over the world through low-cost sustainable methods. A world where farmers face many threats is also a world where some are showing that there are answers. Organic, holistic, sustainable agriculture, still considered a 'fringe' sector by some governments, needs to be scaled up to become mainstream agriculture. Much depends on good practice being replicated widely.

When some talk of a 'new' agriculture they think in terms of high-tech 'solutions' such as genetically modified (GM) foods. This technology could make a contribution but only in the very long term, as Tewolde Egziabher points out in Chapter 6. There are too many issues surrounding GM foods that need to be resolved. New technologies need to be examined in light of their relevance for the world's most undernourished people. In the twenty-first century there are more appropriate technologies than genetic modification and it is those technologies that deserve more attention and funding. This chapter also looks at the role of the influential international agricultural research centres.

Water is the liquid gold that can allow agriculture to thrive. But some wrong turnings have again been taken with irrigation, as Chapter 7 explains. Large dam schemes have been common but are less efficient than small-scale dams. Again there is good news in that the weaknesses of large dam schemes have become apparent. Water harvesting can be important for resource-poor agriculture. And this scarce resource needs to be used and reused more efficiently. 'Water – use it twice' is a good rule whenever possible.

The land available to agriculture is limited and therefore has to be worked carefully and sensitively if it is to produce and continue to produce the food that is needed. The UN Food and Agriculture Organisation (FAO) calculates that only 11 per cent of the world's land area is useful for agriculture, as Chapter 8 makes clear. Improving and sustaining yields on this land is therefore a key task.

Agriculture needs to be 'pro-poor, pro-nature and pro-women', stresses M. S. Swaminathan, the distinguished Indian agriculturalist.[5] Chapter 9 considers how the potential of women food producers can be released, and reviews women's need for greater access to resources and markets, technology, research and extension. This chapter includes a box on the threat to women farmers from genetic engineering. Credit can help small-scale farmers but it can also plunge them into debt; Chapter 10 looks at its potential and pitfalls.

Increased and sustainable food output, even if it comes from resource-poor farmers, is not the whole of the answer to food insecurity. As the experience of a project in Zambia shows in Chapter 11, farmers are often so desperate for cash – to pay education fees for example – that they sell some of their food to raise money. They do not necessarily overcome malnutrition by producing more food. This highlights the close connection between food security and wider factors such as education fees, introduced as part of structural adjustment programmes. Farmers need to be backed up by sound polices for rural development. This chapter also looks at HIV/AIDS, now a serious threat to food output in some of the world's poorest countries.

International trade, especially transnational corporations, the World Trade Organisation, trade liberalisation and World Bank/IMF structural adjustment programmes, have a big impact on Third World agriculture. This is analysed in Chapter 12. A question that receives too little attention is whether more food should stay at home, in developing countries, to feed hungry people, rather than be exported to already well-fed people abroad. Headlines such as 'India desperate to export rice' (*Financial Times*, 21 December 2000) highlight a government's perceived need to earn money from exports rather than to use self-sufficiency to feed its people. While India in theory produces enough staples for all its people, millions of its poorest citizens cannot afford to buy what they need. India therefore exports grain to people who can afford it. This chapter examines the balance between food and export crops.

Climate change, global warming, is not a future threat but a present reality. As Chapter 13 makes clear, climate change is already influencing the type of crops that farmers grow. And prospects for the twenty-first century look bleak. The Intergovernmental Panel on

Climate Change predicts that temperatures globally could rise by up to six degrees this century compared with 0.6 degrees in the last century. The problem could therefore be ten times more severe. This will have profound effects on agriculture and could be detrimental for resource-poor farmers in some of the world's poorest and most vulnerable countries. Other ways in which the environment impacts on agriculture, and agriculture impacts on the environment, are considered in this chapter.

Chapter 14 examines livestock connections, including the meat problem and the overfishing that is denuding the oceans. Official development agencies are considered in the following chapter, with the spotlight especially on the World Bank, the largest development agency. The huge funds the Bank has at its disposal should be radically redirected to help small-farmer agriculture.

It is time for policymakers to give agriculture a new impetus, a new direction, to take it along a road where it can feed the world's hungry, concludes Chapter 16. It can be done and the world knows how to do it.

WAR ON HUNGER?

On 11 September 2001, two planes hijacked by terrorists were deliberately flown into the World Trade Centre in New York, killing around 3,000 people. The world came to a virtual halt. All over the world people stopped what they were doing to watch television or listen to the radio, newspapers were dominated by the atrocity and there was a huge wave of compassion for the people who had died. And the talk was of a war on terrorism, of routing out those responsible for such an evil act.

Also on 11 September 2001, if that day was an average kind of day, around 16,500 children under the age of five died because they were undernourished; their bodies were too weak to survive.[6] That is over five times as many as died in New York, and that is just people aged under five. The world did not come to a halt, newspapers were not dominated by the tragedy and there was no wave of compassion for the bereaved. And there was no talk of a war on the cause of their deaths, of routing out those responsible.

But the following day, on 12 September 2001, another 16,500 children under five died in similar circumstances. Once again, silence. And the following day, and the day after that, the day this book was published, the day that you are reading it.

The people who died in New York died in horrific circumstances. But dying of undernourishment can hardly be pleasant either. It is of course comparatively easy to identify the terrorists responsible for the New York atrocity. It is also necessary to recognise that poverty and hunger are fertile breeding grounds for unrest, and need to be tackled as part of the battle against terrorism. The reasons why people go hungry, why they have so little food that they cannot survive, are complex. But that is no reason for inaction. If the New York atrocity had been five times worse, and if it was repeated every day, the world would really come to a halt until the causes had been dealt with. People dying of undernourishment don't expect that, but they have a right to expect that the world gives their plight more attention, that it is steadfastly determined to rout out and deal with its causes, and to develop a society where the poor live rather than die. Building a new system of agriculture that serves the poor would be a significant boost to that new society. It is my hope that this book will be a contribution.

CHAPTER 2

HISTORICAL PERSPECTIVES

> Loyalty to a petrified opinion never broke a chain or
> freed a human soul.
>
> *Mark Twain*

Agriculture probably began in the Middle East, as described in Chapter 1. It also seems to have started in South America at about the same time with the growing of potatoes and other plants. Around 9,000 years ago, maize (corn) and a variety of other crops, including peppers, avocados and amaranths (leafy vegetables), were domesticated in Central America. Barley appears to have been the prominent crop in agriculture's early days. In China, millet was cultivated 7,000 years ago; rice 2,000 years later.

Wheat, flax, dates, apples, plums and grapes spread in Asia, and the growth of agriculture led to more settled villagers and the rearing of livestock. Domesticated pigs have been recorded in villages in Iraq about 8,750 years ago, domesticated cattle and crops in Greece some 750 years later. Agriculture rather than hunting was practised in areas where soils were fertile, water was abundant and climate was favourable. The spade and the hoe came into use about 6,000 years ago. Bees also seem to have been exploited at an early stage.

Many civilisations, including the ancient Babylonians, Chinese, Egyptians and Hindus, relied extensively on irrigated agriculture. Techniques of harvesting water for agriculture were developed in the Middle East over 3,000 years ago.

Agriculture started later in North America, with peppers, cotton, amaranths, sunflowers and maize spreading from South America about 1,700 years ago. In the Mississippi River drainage basin, 7,000-year-old archaeological evidence indicates that humans began to occupy river flood plains continuously during the summer months. 'This occupation caused disturbances to the flood plain environment that appear to have favored certain weedy invader plants, such as curcubita, goosefoot, sumpweed and sunflower, which have edible seeds. At some undetermined date, humans apparently began to cultivate these plants, and by 3,000 years ago physiological differences had developed between a number of cultivated varieties and their wild relatives'.[1]

Greece seems to have been the first European country to grow crops. From Greece the culture spread to Denmark and Britain, probably about 5,000 years ago. Agriculture in every country was family-oriented, on small plots of land, chiefly for subsistence, developing in ways which suited local conditions, culture and climate. Rotating crops around fields was found to be more profitable – as also was the practice of leaving a field fallow (not used), usually every seven years. It was soon discovered that a crop grown in the same field for even two years in succession did not yield as well in the second year, and that fields benefited from a rest after a number of years.

Traditional systems of agriculture in both northern and southern hemispheres used all the principles of permaculture (permanent agriculture) without necessarily putting a name to it; nutrients were carefully recycled, the waste products of agriculture were fed to livestock, manure was put on the land, and livestock carefully integrated with agriculture.

With the industrial revolution in the eighteenth and nineteenth centuries, traditional systems came under pressure; agriculture became more mechanised and more market-oriented to meet the demand for food from the new industrial towns. But small fields and the rotation principle continued to be the norm in most industrialised countries. In the Third World 'many traditional farming systems were sustainable for centuries in terms of their ability to maintain a continuing, stable level of production'.[2]

But there were crop failures and famines in both poor and rich countries, with factors such as crop disease and the failure of rainfall taking their toll. For example, in China, from 108 BC to 1911 AD, 1,828 famines were recorded – almost one a year.[3]

Soil erosion was another factor in some areas. 'Mayan civilisation seems to have failed after centuries of expansion in Guatemala, because the demands of its growing population depleted the soil through erosion. The shifting sands of Libya and Algeria also testify to the failure of Roman agriculturalists to husband the granary which supplied much of the Roman Empire with food'.[4] It is significant that the failure of agricultural systems led to the collapse of civilisations.

In Europe, probably the most serious famine of the nineteenth century occurred in Ireland, following the infection of the potato crop by a fungus in 1845. The potato was a vital staple food for the country's poor and over a million people died. Their deaths could have been avoided; for Ireland was then exporting maize to Britain, where it seems that people could afford to buy it, unlike starving Irish people. The retention and distribution of that maize in food aid for the starving could have prevented disaster. This type of situation was to become the norm in the late twentieth century: countries with hungry people were exporting food to countries that were able to afford it. Ironically, thirty years later, in 1875, British agriculture was to collapse because of cheap food imports. Again in the late twentieth century, agriculture in developing countries was to come under severe pressure because of cheap food imports, brought about in this case by trade liberalisation.

'TOTAL CHANGE'

The practice of monocropping – the intensive farming of a single crop – first appeared in the North towards the end of the nineteenth century, when prairies in North America were sown to wheat, maize or barley. Monocropping involved a total change in the pattern of agriculture that had been the norm down the centuries Instead of crop rotation and fallow, monocropping depends on fertiliser and pesticides to allow intensive farming of the same land year after year.

The practice spread to Europe and very gradually to the southern hemisphere. By the 1930s the desolate results of prairie-style US agriculture were vividly portrayed in books such as John Steinbeck's *The Grapes of Wrath*.

Under European colonialism of the late nineteenth and early twentieth centuries, the colonised countries were forced to grow export crops for the metropolitan economies. Cecil Rhodes, British promoter of colonialism in the the 1890s, said 'we must find new lands from which we can easily obtain raw materials and at the same time exploit the cheap labour'.[5]

Large areas of land in the Third World were put under coffee, cocoa, sugar, tea, bananas and other crops destined for export. The agricultural pattern in the colonised countries of the Third World changed fundamentally. While food crops sometimes grew alongside the export crops, export crops were often grown on plantations, monoculture style. Chemical fertilisers and pesticides were introduced by companies from the metropolitan economies. Western governments assumed that the intensive agricultural systems that were beginning to work in their countries were also right for developing countries. Traditional farming practices came under threat, as did native peoples. In the Americas, so-called 'New World' diseases carried by explorers from abroad wiped out a large proportion of native populations, who took their knowledge of farming with them to the grave.[6]

There were other pressures too. Traditional farming systems had to cope with rapid changes in agricultural technology, and the introduction of foreign education and health care, plus 'increased population pressures, changes in social and political relationships, and incorporation into an externally-controlled international market system'.[7]

In response to the power and influence of the West, farmers in the Third World tended to change in one of two directions. Some began to use excessive amounts of external inputs. It seemed easier for them to open a bag of fertiliser, for example, than to cart manure and spread it on the land. It seemed more convenient to spray pesticide on crops than to practise the time-honoured but more labour-intensive practice of natural, biological control. For some farmers, the agricultural practices of Western countries had an almost iconic status as 'modern' and this continued in post-colonial days. Most Third World farmers, however, stayed with traditional methods not necessarily out of conviction but because they could not afford or obtain the modern inputs.

But with much of the best land now under export crops, land for food crops came under greater pressure and this often led to their degradation. Land for the long-established practice of shifting cultivation was not as plentiful as before. Growing populations increased the pressure on land. Under shifting cultivation, farmers cultivate an area and then leave it for several years to recover its soil fertility before farming it again. Integral systems of shifting cultivation 'present a good equilibrium between humans and their environment' provided there is sufficient land and no pressure from rising population.[8] Mechanised agriculture expanded over larger areas, replacing the hoe and other hand tools, but ploughs and tractors were often not suited to fragile soils and added to the problems of land degradation.

THE PROBLEM WITH WESTERN-STYLE AGRICULTURE

Monocropping dominates Western-style agriculture (see next chapter for monocropping in developing countries). At the beginning of the twenty-first century, however, this system of agriculture was in crisis. Smaller-scale farmers − those with less than 1,000 acres − increasingly found that they could not make a living from agriculture and their land was being sold to larger entities, often to industrial companies.

The crisis has occurred despite huge subsidies. In 2000 the twenty-nine most industrialised countries belonging to the Organisation for Economic Cooperation and Development paid out US$327 billion in supports and subsidies to farmers.[9] This huge sum − the equivalent of the annual output of Sub-Saharan Africa or nearly the entire public expenditure of Britain − comprised $114.5 billion of EU production support, $54 billion for the USA with the support of all other OECD countries, together with the estimated benefit of tariffs and non-tariff barriers to farmers, making up the remainder. But these supports were of little benefit to small-scale farmers in OECD countries, whose incomes were declining, often sharply. The chief beneficiaries were large-scale agricultural businesses, farming vast areas of land in industrial style. Fields were effectively turned into factories.

Western-style 'modern agriculture' only survives because of these huge subsidies. But economic recession and financial realism mean that money for subsidies is drying up. In Western Europe the Common Agricultural Policy (CAP) was the chief means through which subsidies were paid. Food self-sufficiency in temperate zone foodstuffs was one of the chief original aims of the CAP. In 1945 Europe's food supply relied on massive imports, mainly from the United States; despite relatively high prices to farmers, self-sufficiency in temperate-zone foodstuffs was not achieved until 1974. The CAP effectively gave subsidies to farmers to produce more and this eventually led to surpluses, some of which were stored, some destroyed, some 'dumped' – sold below the cost of production – in developing countries.

Three-quarters of CAP subsidies go to one-quarter of EU farmers – the larger farmers. Smaller farmers, trying to compete, often incurred unpayable debts which drove them into bankruptcy. Their lands were then consolidated into those of the largest and wealthiest farmers. The scale of the collapse was dramatic. Between 1939 and 2000, the number of farms in Britain fell by two-thirds, from almost 500,000 to 158,000; farm incomes fell 72 per cent in the five years to 2000. In Europe, in 1999, 200,000 farmers gave up agriculture.[10]

Many family seed businesses have also been disappearing in Western countries, taken over by larger companies. Diversity was the victim of this consolidation with larger companies specialising in a relatively small numbers of seeds. The availability of local apples in Northern Europe, for example, declined as supermarkets concentrated on a small number of 'standard' varieties.[11]

While increases in crop productivity were occurring in so-called modern, energy- and chemical-intensive agriculture, there was a huge cost. For it was accompanied 'in many instances by environmental degradation (soil erosion, pollution by pesticides, salinization, social problems (elimination of the family farm, concentration of land, resources and production, growth of agribusiness and its dominance over farm production, change in rural/urban migration patterns) and by excessive use of natural resources'.[12]

Many rural areas of Western countries have effectively been turned into silent factories without roofs. Few farm workers are needed on the huge farms that dominate – farms of 5,000 acres may employ only two or three people. But the attempt to control nature in the pursuit of profit has damaged the environment to the point where it is beginning to backfire. Nature is taking revenge.

BSE: Trigger for Change

Western style agriculture was accompanied by Bovine Spongiform Encephalopathy (BSE) – mad cow disease. This developed into an epidemic in Britain because of an unnatural, intensive farming practice, namely feeding processed animal remains to livestock.

BSE was followed in 2001 in Britain by a serious epidemic of foot-and-mouth disease. This appears to have been triggered by imports from Asia and was therefore partly due to the globalisation of the food chain. The centralisation of Britain's abattoirs was also a factor: two-thirds were shut down between 1985 and 2000. Cattle often had to be transported out of their area for slaughtering, increasing the risk of the disease spreading to other areas.

As alarm continued over BSE, German Chancellor Gerhard Schroeder called for a fundamental shift in farm policy away from 'agricultural factories'.[13] This was backed by the European Union's Commissioner for Agriculture, Franz Fischler, who admitted that the BSE crisis 'has taught me that we have to encourage and promote environmentally friendly production methods which respect animal welfare'.[14]

Monoculture, the intensive system of Western agriculture, survives only because it receives large subsidies from government, as described above. It is hardly surprising that farmers have been switching to organic agriculture in record numbers, even though the switch requires a lengthy change-over period, usually five years, so that land is free of chemicals and produce can be certified organic.

Sweden was the first European country to embrace organic agriculture and its farmers are reaping the benefits. In 1987 Sweden banned the use of antibiotics which are used to fatten livestock and rejected the intensive feeding practices that caused BSE in other European countries. 'For ethical reasons Sweden stopped giving ruminants meat', says Lars Hook of the Swedish Farmers Association.[15]

Sweden is now enjoying the fruits of this policy. It has not reported a single case of BSE and demand for meat from domestic consumers has remained buoyant, in contrast to most other European countries. Sweden has massively increased its exports of pigmeat (pork products), especially to Britain – up from 105 tonnes in 1991 to 1,500 tonnes last year.

Other European countries have also been picking up organic speed. By 2001, organic accounted for 10 per cent of agricultural output in Austria and 8 per cent in Switzerland. The USA, France and Japan, were experiencing growth rates of more than 20 per cent annually. The UK market for organic foods increased by 55 per cent during 1999–2000, rising in value to £605 million (from £105 million in 1993). The number of organic farmers in the UK rose from 794 in 1996 to over 2,800 in 2000. By April 2000 there were over 400,000 hectares either under organic or in conversion to organic in the UK, 2.3 per cent of the total agricultural land area. The proportion for the EU as a whole was just under 3 per cent.[16]

The West's mainstream agricultural sectors, meanwhile, have been moving to a situation where there would only be a few thousand farms left, owned by conglomerates and run by managers rather than farmers, or at best farmed on a contract basis. Small-scale farmers in Western countries who are surviving are more likely to be farming organically, even though they receive less support from government.

The effects of spreading such 'modern' agriculture to developing countries are now clear. In China the modernisation of agriculture has already led to the uprooting of more than half the rural population in the last two decades. Pastoralists in West Africa have been displaced by cheap meat imports from Europe, while Indian farmers – who grow traditional oilseeds like sesame, linseed, and mustard – are being driven under by soya imported from the US. Mexican beef producers are losing ground to US producers, whose inroads into Mexico's markets have tripled since the North American Free Trade Agreement (NAFTA) was ratified.

Rural communities in both developed and developing countries are therefore facing hardship and decline. Unprecedented numbers of farmers are confronting insurmountable financial burdens, and some – from British shepherds to Indian cotton farmers – are seeing suicide as their only way out.

In Andhra Pradesh, India, for example, a series of suicides among peasant farmers began with cotton producers who, encouraged by the promise of high returns, planted large areas with a single cotton hybrid that proved to be particularly susceptible to insect attack. Faced with uncontrollable pest outbreaks and insurmountable loans, many farmers resorted to killing themselves by drinking the insecticide intended for their fields.[17]

Western-style agriculture, with its costly machinery, is intensive in its use of energy, especially oil. If total world agricultural production and food processing were based on European and North American levels of energy use, says George McRobie, co-founder of the Intermediate Technology Development Group, 'known oil reserves would disappear off the face of the earth in 30 years. If we hook farmers in developing countries into a Western style of agriculture, then they are doomed because it is not sustainable and the environment can't stand it'.[18] Energy- and chemicals-intensive agriculture is inherently unsustainable. A report, sponsored by the World Bank, found that many water sources are being polluted by the excessive use of fertilisers and pesticides. Agricultural productivity and food supplies are at risk, it warned, because of increasing water scarcity and soil degradation.[19]

LEARNING FROM WHOM?

Agriculture is more than just another industry. Western-style agriculture has neglected the principles of traditional husbandry, turned farms into factories and driven small farmers from their land. It is intensive in its use of fertilisers, pesticides, water and energy to the point of causing serious damage. It is not suitable for Western let alone developing countries. It has certainly no moral right to be considered a model for countries in the South to follow.

Western countries need fundamentally to rethink their agriculture and regain some of the practices that have largely been lost, such as mixed cropping, traditional husbandry and the use of natural rather than artificial fertilisers. Western governments are beginning to talk about the need for sustainable agriculture; they could usefully pick up some of the best ideas of Third World agriculture which are often highly sustainable. It is sustainable systems that are 'the way forward for the Western world'.[20] While much traditional knowledge has been lost, we have now entered an age where the amount of information spreading around the world through the Internet is growing at a prodigious rate. This includes knowledge about traditional farming systems that could provide the food the world needs.

CHAPTER 3

THIRD WORLD AGRICULTURE: WHO GROWS WHAT?

Are we willing and able to accept a poor, illiterate third world farmer as our teacher?

Hans Carlier

About 1,500 million people in developing countries make a living from small-scale farming under a wide range of climatic and physical conditions. Overwhelmingly resource-poor, these farmers have small plots of land, often in marginal areas, where rainfall is inadequate, and soils fragile and vulnerable to erosion. On these small plots farmers grow a wide variety of crops, balanced in the light of experience, that yield varying degrees of return – from the good downwards. Mostly growing food crops, some also grow crops for export, often for a pittance. Some keep poultry and small ruminants, such as sheep and goats. Many farmers produce food entirely for their own family's subsistence, others sell some of their output on local, national and international markets.

Despite the problems, including inadequate markets for inputs and produce, many of these smallholders succeed in running viable operations. Others are unable to grow enough food to last their families for a whole year and several hungry months of the year may result. Raising food output on these farms is an important part of the 'end hunger' jigsaw.

According to FAO figures compiled from national census statistics, Asia has around 385 million farms, Africa 36 million, Central America 6 million, South America 10 million. There are therefore approximately 437 million farms in developing countries, from which 1,500 million people make a living.[1] While most small-scale farms are cultivated by traditional methods, a substantial number, possibly over 40 per cent, have adopted chemically intensive, 'modern' Western-style agricultural methods.

CROPS FOR FOOD

Staple foods cover about 62 per cent of the arable area of developing countries and are especially important to the poor. Resource-poor people will save food when they can for use in times of hardship, but normal harvests may allow for only a limited amount to be stored. 'Poor people typically save in good seasons but run down their reserves in lean times. Overall their consumption is seldom much below their income'.[2] Wheat, rice and maize are the chief crops grown for food in developing countries, providing over 80 per cent of intake.

Wheat The world's main cereal crop in terms of output. Once restricted to countries in temperate and sub-tropical zones, wheat is now planted out as a winter crop in hotter climates. Wheat requires less water than rice, it has a shorter growing time and greater flexibility. It also has relatively few natural insect enemies and a strong built-in resistance to major diseases, so helping to assure farmers of stable yields. Wheat is unique in that unlike other cereals its kernel contains a gluten protein that makes it possible to produce a wide array of end products. Most of the wheat sown in developing countries is wheat to make bread, with China, India and Turkey the leading producers. Durum wheat – used to make pasta and other products – grows chiefly in the Middle East, Central India, West Asia and North Africa.

In the last two decades of the twentieth century, average yields in developing countries almost doubled, to average 2.5 tonnes per hectare, although higher-yielding varieties are slowing down. In marginal environments yields may be less than 1 t/ha. 'Wheat is expected to become the number one grain in developing countries'.[3]

But as the developing world's output of the crop is currently less than half the world total output, it may be some time before wheat becomes its leading grain.

Rice (paddy) The developing world's main cereal crop, rice, is the staple food for around half of humanity. Over 90 per cent of rice is grown and eaten in Asia, with China, India and Indonesia the dominant producers. The crop is grown, mostly by small-scale farmers, in five different ecosystems: irrigated, rain-fed lowland, upland, deep water and tidal lowland. High-yielding varieties of rice, developed in the 1960s' 'Green Revolution' have only benefited farmers with irrigation. About 40 per cent of the area under rice in Asia is not irrigated and farmers have seen no benefit. Average rice yields are about 3.5 tonnes per hectare, again much lower in marginal environments.[4]

Maize The staple food for about 200 million people, mostly in Africa and Latin America, maize has replaced millet, and also sorghum, in some dryland areas. Improved varieties that can withstand heat and drought are making it possible for maize to grow where it was previously avoided. But many varieties wither if they are not watered at the right time; this can make the crop a gamble for farmers without irrigation.

Other important food crops grown by farmers in developing countries are:

Cassava A root crop, cassava grows in many developing countries and is a staple food for over 200 million people. Considered vital for food security because of its reliability, cassava grows well on marginally fertile soils and yields well when unfavourable climatic conditions cause cereal and pulse crops to fail. In Sub-Saharan Africa, cassava produces more food energy per unit of cultivated land than any other staple crop and provides an inexpensive source of carbohydrates. Cassava's edible, tuberous roots can be left unharvested in the ground up to four years, which makes it an ideal reserve crop when other crops fail; this has led to the saying: 'Where there is cassava, there is no hunger'.

Millet Pearl millet is the chief staple food for around 100 million people. Grown very largely by the poorest of the poor on small plots, it can survive in shallow, sandy, desert-like soil where other crops will not grow. Usually watered only by rainfall, the crop can survive in dry areas with less than 400 mm of rain a year. But yields are often low and the preparation time for cooking is lengthy. In Africa, pearl millet grows in the Sahel, the Sudan zone, most countries in east Africa and in the south in Malawi, Mozambique, Namibia, Zambia and Zimbabwe. In Asia it grows chiefly in India, but also in China, Nepal and Pakistan. It is known as an 'orphan crop' because it has been largely neglected in agricultural research.

Potato One of the most important and versatile food crops in both developed and developing countries. More than one-third of global potato output is now coming from developing countries. It is especially popular in Latin America where it originated. In the Third World it is grown mostly by resource-poor farmers using breeding lines specifically designed for developing-country conditions.

Banana An essential part of the daily diet for communities in more than 100 tropical and subtropical countries. It is grown for food on small plots in many countries and as an export crop in others, on both small plots and plantations. In Africa it is often intercropped with other staples on garden plots, for local use. In the Caribbean, banana grows on hillsides, in Latin America on plantations for export.

Vegetables Hugely important in developing countries, and grown mainly in garden plots, they provide essential nutrients and are often the only food available during the lean season or if the main harvest fails. The last twenty years have also seen a big increase in the export of certain vegetables – from Latin America to the United States for example.[5]

CROPS FOR EXPORT

Growing crops destined for the export market takes up land on which food crops for hungry local people could grow, but, at the same time, it yields a cash income. There is little doubt, however, that an expansion of land under export crops 'is likely to lead to a decline in nutritional standards unless food systems are developed to provide adequate supplies of food at appropriate prices throughout the year. Cash crop policy needs to be closely related to food policy'.[6]

Such an expansion of land under export crops took place in the 1990s, fuelled by structural adjustment programmes (SAPs) and especially by trade liberalisation. SAPs encouraged governments to give greater incentives to farmers to produce crops for export. But this often reduced the priority that governments gave to their food crop sector and led to more land and resources being devoted to export crops and less to domestic food production. In Benin, for example, government incentives led to an increase in land under cotton; cotton exports increased to the detriment of food security.[7]

The crucial factor is the prices these crops fetch on the export market, and whether the prices give the grower a reasonable return (see Chapter 12). While governments are according more priority to the export crop sector, this does not necessarily mean that farmers are receiving better prices for these crops. World prices for many of the developing world's export crops were touching historically low levels in 2001. And with widespread privatisation, it is traders rather than government bodies who are now mostly buying these crops from the farmer. Whoever the buyer, the price offered to the farmer will be related, in some degree, to the world price. But such is the power of traders in some countries that the price the farmer receives may be far below the world price.

Among the chief crops grown for export are:

Coffee Traditionally the developing world's second largest primary commodity earner after oil, coffee is grown by around 10 million people in 80 countries, with Brazil by far the largest producing country. Around 70 per cent of coffee growers are small-scale farmers. In Africa, Asia and parts of Latin America, coffee is grown on small plots. Also in Latin America it grows on plantations. In 2001 the world price of coffee reached its lowest point for 30 years, well below the cost of producing coffee. The way the coffee market works means that growers often get a meagre return even when prices rise.

Most coffee is traded down a line of dealers before it is exported; it can change hands as much as 150 times.

Cocoa Most cocoa is grown in West Africa, Brazil and Indonesia. Around 1.2 million people grow the crop, mostly smallholder resource-poor farmers, although some cocoa grows on plantations. About 11 million people are estimated to be dependent on the crop, which is sold mostly as raw beans to manufacturers of chocolate in Western countries. Prices are again close to record-low levels.

Sugar Grown in over 50 developing countries, sugar cane cultivation ranges from mostly plantation style in the Caribbean to small plots in the Philippines. Cane sugar competes with beet sugar grown in the West and in the recent past has given growers a poor return, with the world prices again at very low levels. A limited amount of sugar from the African, Caribbean and Pacific (ACP) group has enjoyed preferential access to the European Union for which ACP farmers have received high prices, in line with European growers.

Cotton Grown in 60 mostly developing countries, cotton is produced under a range of techniques ranging from smallholder plots, the norm in Sub-Saharan Africa, to large-scale irrigated schemes in central Asia. Cotton has the advantage of being an annual crop, allowing farmers to decide how much to plant next year, for example, based on their return from the crop this year. It has the disadvantage of being environmentally destructive, taking a quarter of the world's pesticides. Organically grown cotton is now showing that farmers can dispense with pesticides.

Rubber More than 80 per cent of rubber is grown in the two leading rubber-producing countries, Thailand and Indonesia, and comes from smallholders. Malaysia, India and China are other leading producers. A number of West African countries also grow rubber. Returns are again low, with the long-term price trend downward.

Tobacco This controversial crop is grown in around 75 developing countries, usually by smallholders on a contract basis. In Kenya, for example, the transnational company British American Tobacco (BAT) contracts 17,500 smallholders to grow tobacco on plots of half a hectare to one hectare. The growing season is lengthy and returns are generally meagre. Possibly more than any other export crop, tobacco poses a direct threat to food security, taking up land on which food could grow, and causing damage to land, owing to the large volume of trees that are needed in the tobacco curing process.

The Methods:
Intercropping versus Monocropping

Traditional forms of cultivation

In the eighteenth century, Thomas Barnard studied agricultural output in 800 villages spread over several districts of India. He found that the average production of paddy was 3,600 kg per hectare, with the best 130 villages averaging 8,200 kg per hectare. This is higher than the average yields that farmers were to obtain two centuries later under the so-called 'Green Revolution' of the 1960s. 'Bernard put this abundance down to optimal seed selection to suit the site, sophistication yet simplicity of tools, extreme care in tending the fields, and techniques such as intercropping and fallow'.[8]

Intercropping, also known as mixed cropping, or polyculture (as opposed to monoculture), has a long and successful history. Resource-poor farmers down the centuries have evolved intercropping systems to produce the food they needed. They were aware that cropping technologies had to be in balance with nature and not denude the soil's nutrients, and were often highly innovative. Trying to develop a system best suited to their land, they experimented with different mixes of crops, learned the best ways to ward off pests, found ways of coping with harsh weather and generally developed a way of farming that worked for them in a sustainable manner. Most traditional farmers employed practices 'designed to optimise productivity in the long term rather than maximise it in the short term'.[9] Ecological methods, including organic manures and biological pest control, lie at the heart of the many thousands of traditional systems.

Farmers are able to draw on a long experience of traditional agriculture and benefit from 'centuries of cultural and biological evolution that has adapted it to local conditions'.[10] They continue today to develop complex farming systems that help them meet their needs even under adverse environmental conditions – on marginal soils, in drought- or flood-prone areas, with scarce resources – without depending on mechanisation or chemical fertilisers.

Yet their agriculture is dismissed by modernists as 'primitive', 'backward', 'low productivity', something in need of change. The reality is that productivity per hectare can be higher than under 'modern' agriculture. 'Small ecological farms have productivity hundreds of times higher than large industrial farms based on conventional farms', says Vandana Shiva.[11]

Intercropping has logical advantages. Among the benefits are that it results 'in more efficient utilisation of resources (light, water, nutrients) by plants of different height, canopy structure and nutrient requirements ... provides insurance against crop failure, especially in areas subject to frost, flood and drought ... provides effective cover to soil and reduces the loss of soil moisture ... and the shading provided by complex crop canopies helps to suppress weeds'. It may also mean that pests and disease are kept under control.[12] (See Chapter 13 for a discussion on soils.)

Growing and rotating two or more crops on the same land also allows the crops to support each other in warding off pests.

This type of agriculture is biotechnology in its broadest sense as it makes use of bio-resources. In the late 1990s the word 'biotechnology' became too closely equated with genetic modification. But GM technology is only one of thousands of biotechnologies. Sound biotechnology always builds on farmers' knowledge, however, which GM technology fails to do.[13]

'Modern' agriculture

Traditional farming systems came under attack in the post-World War Two era, with chemical companies and government departments leading the way in persuading small farmers to switch to 'modern' agriculture. Support for the 'modern' school also comes

28   FOOD FOR ALL

from groups 'within the World Bank, Winrock International, FAO and the Sasakawa Global 2000 project in Africa'.[14]

The approach requires high technology, chemical fertilisers, high-yielding seeds, irrigation, and labour-saving machinery, leading to a decline in the number of jobs for local people. Farmers were told they could get higher yields with much less effort – from a bag of chemicals, for example, rather than from applied knowledge. With this high-tech approach, many decisions were taken out of the hands of farmers and local people, thus decreasing local self-reliance and confidence. The approach also shifted economic opportunity and decision-making to men and away from women, despite the fact that women, especially in Africa, produce most of the food.

In the 1960s, monocropping became synonymous with 'modern' agriculture. The associated 'Green Revolution' led to spectacular increases in yields of rice and wheat, at least initially, and to the rapid spread of this type of agriculture. The monocropping of fields with a single crop is efficient, claim its advocates, allowing for economies of scale, permitting each crop to be grown on the soil best suited to it, and giving maximum yields and returns to farmers. 'About half the rice, wheat and maize areas in Third World countries are planted to modern varieties, and fertiliser and pesticide consumption has grown rapidly'.[15] The use of nitrogen fertiliser increased from 2 million tonnes (m.t.) in 1940 to 75 m.t. in 1995. While mixed cropping was sometimes retained under 'modern agriculture', often it gave way to monocropping.

Although most resource-poor farmers in developing countries could not afford the inputs necessary for monocropping, millions were nonetheless persuaded. And after seeing yields rise, following early applications of fertilisers, the traditional techniques were scorned. The disadvantages of monocropping have slowly become apparent. Under monocropping, farmers are dependent on chemical insecticides, disease-resistant plant varieties, soil fumigation and similar methods of controlling insects and diseases that were traditionally controlled by crop rotation. Yields in many areas are declining – in India's green revolution belt, for example, wheat and rice yields are declining to uneconomic levels. Diseases are spreading. Mono-

cropping universally attracts pests, which usually need to be controlled by expensive chemicals; it slowly degrades the soil and is usually
unsustainable. Ironically pesticides – which make monocropping possible – are also losing their effectiveness.

By concentrating on a few varieties of crops, monocropping has
led to a serious loss of diversity, especially to the replacement of local
crop variety. 'As history has tragically shown, planting a large area
with a single cultivar (of a crop) can result not only in extreme
susceptibility to new strains of a pathogen or pest, but also in
catastrophic loss of genetic diversity', points out Miguel Altieri.[16] A
diverse variety of plants, both wild and cultivated, is essential if crops
are to be developed that yield more, resist pests and disease, and
tolerate difficult environments. 'The growing dependence on a narrow
range of species increases vulnerability to disasters such as pest attack,
crop disease or drought. The loss of these diverse systems can also
reduce farmers' food security by reducing the variety of available
foods'.[17]

The apparent benefits from monoculture, in terms of yields, are
also misleading. Planting one crop in an entire field may increase its
individual yield, while planting multiple crops in a mixture will have
low yields of individual crops but a higher total output of food.
Studies suggest that monocropping is less productive than mixed
cropping. Shiva cites a study of a polyculture system which found
that 'you need 5 units of inputs to produce 100 units of food. That's
a productivity of 20. For monoculture you need 300 units of input
to produce 100 units of food. That's a productivity as low as 0.33'.[18]
To the farmer it is overall output that matters.

Once farmers have made the switch from mixed cropping to
monocropping, knowledge of the systems which have worked for
decades, even centuries, can easily be lost. 'I discovered when I
worked in Latin America that it took just one generation for all
farming knowledge to be lost in a community', says Howard
Shapiro, one of the founders of a US-based organisation 'Seeds of
Change'.[19] 'The real tragedy of the green revolution is that it undermined, and in many cases destroyed, farmers' practices based on
diversity'.[20]

The result is that humankind has now become dangerously dependent on a small number of crops. 'The genetic diversity of our critical plant species is disappearing at a terrible pace', says a report by the Crucible Group, made up of experts from poor and rich countries.[21] Over the last 100 years, around three-quarters of the world's known plant species have been lost. There were 30,000 varieties of rice growing in India at the start of the twentieth century; today around three-quarters of India's rice crops comes from ten varieties. According to the Global Biodiversity Assessment of the United Nations Environment Programme, 5 to 20 per cent of plant species are threatened with extinction in the foreseeable future, unless present trends are reversed.[22]

Increasingly it appears that monocropping is not consistent with sustainable agriculture, and that high-tech 'modern agriculture' is failing to achieve food security in developing countries. The modernists 'ignore the evidence of the last 50 years … it is becoming increasingly clear that not only is this approach failing to improve food security for the most vulnerable, it has also been achieved at great environmental cost, to the extent that production levels through these approaches in many areas have now stagnated, or are even declining … and that the practice is very costly and causes a lot of damage to the environment', believes Jules Pretty.[23] Some farmers are now recovering and developing traditional techniques (see Chapter 5), abandoning new crop varieties because of the high cost of inputs and disappointing returns.

WISDOM, NOT CHEMICALS

The application of knowledge rather than chemicals is the key to increasing food output on small farms in developing countries. Mixed cropping has a proven success as a strategy that can both produce the food that is needed immediately, and is sustainable. 'It is now increasingly recognised that indigenous farming systems, based on mixed cropping, soil and water conservation and biological pest management … can produce more output and a wider range of harvested products, particularly in marginal environments'.[24] Third World agriculture has taken some wrong turns in the past century. Commercial pressures may try to direct it down blind but temporarily profitable alleyways, for the sake of the companies rather than of the farmers. Resisting those pressures is one of the challenges on the road to overcoming hunger.

CHAPTER 4

THE HUNGRY

Give me neither poverty not riches, but give me only
my daily bread.

Book of Proverbs, 30:8

'Give me bread, let it be burnt or stale, it kills the fire in
my stomach', runs a prayer from a hungry person in India.
'In exchange, take whatever you like. I could surrender
the freedom of my country for bread. With just two pieces
of bread I can start my day before sunrise. I can shake
out the knotted hair of the stormy sea. Love, sadness,
thought, I set at nothing. I would give all for bread'.

Anon.

'I didn't have any breakfast and walked around half dizzy. The daze
of hunger is worse than that of alcohol. The daze of alcohol makes
us sing but the one of hunger makes us shake. I know how horrible
it is to have only air in the stomach', writes a Brazilian slum dweller.[1]
Poverty is the chief reason why people go hungry; they do not have
access to enough food, they are too poor to grow enough or to buy
enough food, they do not have the money to exercise effective demand in the market. Their poverty is often directly related to agriculture. For it is in agriculture where most of the poor strive to earn
their living, often with limited access to resources such as land,
water, credit and markets. Millions of the poor are either landless or
have only small plots of land, many live far away from roads, making
inputs for agriculture difficult to obtain and markets difficult to reach.

In most rural areas, there are few jobs outside agriculture and the growth rate in rural non-farm employment is low. This means that few have the chance to earn a wage that enables them to buy the food they need. People can go hungry in villages where local markets are brimming over with food.

Poverty needs to be tackled on many levels. Developing countries need fundamental changes in the international economic system. Changes in the national economies of most developing countries are needed to give priority to overcoming poverty; and changes in the rural economy are needed to provide more jobs and income for the majority who live in rural areas. The right kind of agriculture, one that works for the poor, would contribute greatly to conquering poverty.

WHO ARE THE HUNGRY?

Hunger stunts the lives of people and the prosperity of nations. FAO studies suggest that hunger costs developing countries up to US$128 billion per year in productivity losses alone. But the human cost is far higher. Without adequate food, people cannot lead healthy, active lives. Hunger dulls intellects and thwarts productivity, keeping people and communities from realising their potential. Hunger and micro-nutrient deficiencies are estimated to decrease children's learning capacity by up to 10 per cent. For poor families in developing countries, hunger-related illness adds to household costs and increases the burden of care for healthy family members.

In terms of numbers, there are more chronically hungry people in Asia, but the depth of hunger is greatest in Sub-Saharan Africa, where the undernourished have an average deficit of more than 300 kilocalories per person per day. The depth of hunger is measured by comparing the average amount of dietary energy that undernourished people get from the foods they eat with the minimum amount of dietary energy they need to maintain body weight and undertake light activity. On average, the 800 million plus chronically hungry people worldwide lack 100–400 kilocalories per day.[2]

Eighteen of the 23 countries facing the most severe problems in feeding their people are African. Afghanistan, Bangladesh, Haiti, Mongolia and North Korea make up the list. South Asia contains 284 million chronically hungry people; East and Southeast Asia, 242 million; Sub-Saharan Africa, 180 million; Latin America, 53 million; Near East and North Africa, 33 million.[3] The incidence of poverty is particularly high among indigenous populations, some 250 million people.

> Lack of cash income is one of the most important factors hindering both urban and rural people from obtaining the diverse foods needed for an adequate diet. Even when poor rural families are helped to produce a greater variety of foods on their household plots, they will often sell these items rather than consume them because of their high market value.[4]

Hunger results not so much from insufficient food supplies 'as from people's lack of access to those supplies'.[5] The problem is therefore not lack of food in the world overall or even the productive capacity to produce the food that is needed. If the food produced in the world 'were to be divided equally among its inhabitants, every man, woman and child would consume 2,760 kilocalories each day', points out FAO Director-general Jacques Diouf.[6]

THE INTERNATIONAL COMMITMENT

In the last big summit of the twentieth century, leaders of 186 countries met in Rome in November 1996 for the World Food Summit. Around 840 million people were then estimated to be chronically hungry. Leaders ended the Summit by approving the Rome Declaration on World Food Security and Plan of Action to combat hunger, making a commitment to halve the number of hungry people in the world by 2015, as a first step to the goal of food for all. The cost would amount to US$60 billion over 15 years, or US$4 billion per year in increased spending. The declaration states:

> We, the Heads of State and Government, or our representatives, reaffirm the right of everyone to have access to safe and nutritious food, consistent with the right to adequate food and the fundamental right of everyone to be free from hunger … we pledge our political will and our common and national commitment to achieving food security for all and to an on-

going effort to eradicate hunger in all countries, with an immediate view to reducing the number of undernourished people to half their present level no later than 2015. We consider it intolerable that more than 800 million people throughout the world, and particularly in developing countries, do not have enough food to meet their basic nutritional needs. This situation is unacceptable ... The problems of hunger and food insecurity have global dimensions and are likely to persist, and even increase dramatically in some regions, unless urgent, determined and concerted action is taken, given the anticipated increase in the world's population and the stress on natural resources.

Food security is defined in the declaration as: 'Food that is available at all times, to which all persons have means of access, that is nutritionally adequate in terms of quantity, quality and variety, and is acceptable within the given culture'.

The declaration recognises that the limited access of rural women to productive resources and their restricted role in policy and economic decision-making contribute to poverty and are obstacles to food security; that policies and programmes in many countries pay little heed to equality between men and women, and that the absence of gender-disaggregated information and data prevents informed social and economic decision-making.

In the Plan of Action, leaders make seven commitments:

1. We will ensure an enabling political, social, and economic environment designed to create the best conditions for the eradication of poverty and for durable peace, based on full and equal participation of women and men, which is most conducive to achieving sustainable food security for all.
2. We will implement policies aimed at eradicating poverty and inequality and improving physical and economic access by all, at all times, to sufficient, nutritionally adequate and safe food and its effective utilisation.
3. We will pursue participatory and sustainable food, agriculture, fisheries, forestry and rural development policies and practices in high and low potential areas, which are essential to adequate and reliable food supplies at the household, national, regional and global levels, and combat pests, drought and desertification, considering the multifunctional character of agriculture.
4. We will strive to ensure that food, agricultural trade and overall trade policies are conducive to fostering food security for all through a fair and market-oriented world trade system.
5. We will endeavour to prevent and be prepared for natural disasters and man-made emergencies and to meet transitory and emergency food

requirements in ways that encourage recovery, rehabilitation, development and a capacity to satisfy future needs.

6. We will promote optimal allocation and use of public and private investments to foster human resources, sustainable food, agriculture, fisheries and forestry systems, and rural development, in high and low potential areas.

7. We will implement, monitor, and follow-up this Plan of Action at all levels in cooperation with the international community.

The commitments made at the World Food Summit are both limited and bold – limited because poverty and hunger need to be abolished not halved, and because they are not binding on governments. But the commitments are also bold. Halving hunger has never been done before. If it is achieved, and it must be achieved, it would mark a historic step on the way to food for all. But for the commitment to be translated into reality, more priority and resources will be needed. The commitment is therefore an important marker. Governments are expected to keep it; the world is watching to see that they do.

SINCE THE WORLD FOOD SUMMIT

Progress in the years after the World Food Summit (WFS) has been disappointing. The first two years of the post-WFS era were also marked by financial turmoil in Asia, which threatened to reverse some of the economic gains made by Asian countries in the fight against hunger. Millions of people lost their jobs and livelihoods in the economic downturn; they returned to rural communities that had been used to receiving a part of their urban wages. People had to cope with soaring prices of basic foodstuffs and agricultural inputs, again caused by the crisis. In Indonesia, the percentage of people living below the poverty line declined from 60 per cent in 1970 to 11 per cent in 1996. But between 1996 and the end of 1998, 10 million people lost their jobs in the financial crisis and poverty increased sixfold. The people worst affected were inevitably the most food insecure.

In November 1998, an FAO paper warned that 'progress is not being made at anywhere near the rates required for meeting the

WFS target. Unless major efforts are made to improve food supplies, as well as to overcome inequalities, some countries may still have an incidence of undernutrition ranging from 15 to 30 per cent of their populations'. The world has the capacity to produce the additional food needed to eliminate undernutrition, the paper went on, and 'The persistence of hunger is due to development failures'.[7]

In October 1999, the FAO's *The State of Food Insecurity in the World 1999* stated: 'Since 1990/92, the number of people going hungry in developing countries has declined by 40 million. Malnourishment fell in 37 countries between 1990/92 and 1995/97'. The report noted that some regions had made impressive progress over the past two decades, demonstrating that hunger is not an intractable problem.[8]

A year later, the FAO's next report on food insecurity noted that 826 million people were chronically hungry and that the rate of decline in the number of hungry people was woefully inadequate, reducing by only 8 million per year during the first half of the 1990s – a reduction of at least 20 million every year between 2000 and 2015 being needed to reach the WFS target. Unless extra efforts were made to accelerate progress, the 1996 WFS goal of cutting the number of undernourished to 400 million by 2015 would not be achieved before 2030 – 15 years late. This lack of progress underlined 'the urgency of immediate, determined and truly effective action', the report stressed; 'hungry people cannot wait another 15 years'.[9]

But another FAO report, the findings of a study on global warming, makes for disturbing reading. It suggests that climate change will cause severe drought conditions in parts of Africa by 2050. An additional 30 million Africans could therefore be affected by famine, 'because of the reduced inability to grow crops in large parts of Africa'.[10] If this calculation is correct, the international community will have to increase sharply its assistance to enable Africa to cope with the threat.

The rate of agricultural growth has again been disappointing, with the years since the WFS witnessing a slowdown in most developing countries. In 1997 output expanded by 2.9 per cent, in 1998 by 2.6 per cent, but it dropped only 1 per cent in 1999, 'the lowest recorded rate of growth in agricultural production in the developing countries since 1972'.[11]

Worse was to come, however. In 2000, cereal output in Asia fell by 4.5 per cent, chiefly because of adverse growing conditions and a decrease in planted area in China. In developing countries as a whole, cereal output fell from 1,232.3 million tonnes to 1,185.3 m.t – a 3.8 per cent drop.

'Developing country yields in main food crops are crawling up at one-third the pace of the 1970s … Why? Do globalisation, technical change or scale economies destroy small-farm advantage and with it most of the hope of poverty reduction?', asks Professor Michael Lipton of the UK's University of Sussex. He concludes that it is the interlocking of these factors with the 'public-goods problem … that is deeply threatening for small farms'. Publicly funded agricultural research, for example, is becoming increasingly privatised. The delivery of services such as water is being concentrated unduly 'on the needs of rich, big, capitally intensive farmers'.[12] This highlights the importance of small farms in reducing poverty and growing the food that is needed to meet the 2015 target. Small farmers are more likely to grow the staple foods on which the poor depend. Post-1950 poverty reductions 'are all small-farm based', points out Lipton; 'if small farms dwindle, poverty won't fall much'.[13]

Yet many governments of developing countries continue to pursue policies favouring the big rather than the small farmer. When support for small farmers is given it can include the use of subtle persuasion to apply chemicals on their crops. Agricultural extension workers in Ethiopia, for example, are given a quota of farmers they have to try to persuade each month to use chemical fertilisers on their land. As many have to get into debt to buy the fertiliser the policy has economic as well as environmental dangers.

The FAO predicts that world agricultural output will pick up and grow by 1.6 per cent a year to 2015, outstripping predicted world population growth of 1.1 per cent a year – a deceleration that will contribute to a slowing down in the demand for food. Cereals will remain the principal source of food supplies, accounting for about half of daily calorie intakes. But developing countries will become increasingly dependent on imports of cereals.

Agricultural Poverty

Shashore Shamana is a widow with four children who farms just over half an acre of land around her home near Sodo in south-west Ethiopia. She grows maize, sweet potato and banana and has a few coffee trees. The coffee berries, like the other produce, are solely for consumption by herself and her four children.

In a normal year, a year when the rain comes, the food that Shashore Shamana grows is enough to feed the family for five months of the year. She has no irrigation; rain provides the only water for her crops, as it does for most farmers in Ethiopia. But maize does not grow unless there is rain, and in drought years – and 2000 was a drought year in the area – there may be enough food from the land for only three months. 'When the rains fail, we suffer a lot', she says.

How does she survive in the other months of the year? 'I collect wood from the forest and sell it for 1.5 birr a bundle (about 12p). If I can sell two bundles a day, I can buy enough food to feed the family'.

There has been some improvement in the family's health, says Shashore, because she now has clean water which flows down a nearby pipeline, laid under a project run by a local voluntary organisation, Action for Development. With clean water, Shashore's family is more fortunate than many; otherwise with no money and very few material assets, Shashore is a farmer at the heart of agricultural poverty.

'I have no expectations of the future', she says. People like Shashore Shamana are being virtually bypassed by the international community and national governments. Research into agricultural development has not started with their problems. International trade is hardly relevant. A reduction in Ethiopia's debt burden would release money for government spending to combat poverty and help resource-poor agriculture.

Source: Interview with author, March 2001.

And Now?

In November 2001, government ministers were due to meet again for a World Food Summit+Five to assess progress towards achieving the goal that was set in 1996. But because of the international situation the meeting was postponed until June 2002.

In May 2001 an FAO preparatory paper for the World Food Summit+Five charged both developing and developed countries with failing 'to demonstrate their commitment to set aside the resources required to achieve the eradication of hunger in all its dimensions ... Despite a strong global consensus that the main goal for development must be the elimination of poverty, and that lack of access to adequate food is the most appalling manifestation of poverty, there has been a conspicuous lack of focus within poverty reduction strategies on food security issues', says the paper; 'concern over hunger tends to be confined largely to highly visible emergency situations, but the bulk of the world's undernourished people face food shortages day-in, day-out throughout their lives'.[14]

At the June 2002 meeting, governments are likely to reaffirm their commitment to the 2015 target and launch a 'Trust Fund for Food Security' with an initial amount of US$500 million to support developing country agriculture.

This seems unlikely to be enough, however, and the hunger problem 'may get worse before it gets better', warns Indian scientist, M.S. Swaminathan, 'neither global nor macro-economic policies are in favour'.[15] Many governments do not yet have the policies to match their commitments, while the international economic environment is hardly favourable.

According to FAO, a number of factors are of key importance in overcoming hunger: improving access to food, growth with equity, food and agricultural production, building technological capital, developing human capital, sound and stable institutions, making incentives work and 'keeping pace with globalization'.[16]

Higher food output where it is needed is important but does not automatically mean increased food security. 'What is also important is who produces the food, who has access to the technology and knowledge to produce it and who has the purchasing power to acquire it'.[17] Increased investment in the rural economy to raise cash incomes; as well as in the provision of education, clean water and sanitation; and improved health and social services, can all help to reduce the incidence of hunger.

CHAPTER 5

THE NEW AGRICULTURE

A revolution is taking shape in developing-country agriculture. The assumption that monoculture gives high yields, and that diversity means low productivity, is being seriously challenged (see Chapter 3). A growing number of small-scale farmers are showing that the future lies not with monocropping and chemical farming but with organic and semi-organic methods, many of which involve the recovery and integration of traditional technologies. Small biodiverse farms, growing a number of crops in the same field, are proving to be the new agriculture that is more likely to grow the food that is needed by this and future generations.

This new Green Revolution is still to make a breakthrough, however, in the minds of many policymakers and agricultural advisors, who cling to the belief that the chemical route is the best way forward. In many countries, agroecology remains a sleeping partner.

In other countries, however, the 'partner' is waking up with dramatic effects. 'Agroecological techniques can enable small farmers throughout the world to produce much of the food they need ... [given] increasing evidence and awareness of the advantages offered through agroecology, why isn't it being adopted more widely?', asks Miguel Altieri. The challenge, he says, 'is to find ways to increase investment and research in agroecology and to scale up agroecological processes that have already proven successful'.[1]

Sustainable Agriculture

In the 1990s specific examples of sustainable agriculture began to be collated and disseminated. Sustainable farming

> makes the best use of nature's goods and services whilst not damaging the environment. It does this by integrating natural processes such as nutrient cycling, nitrogen fixation, soil regeneration and natural enemies of pests into food production processes. It minimises the use of non-renewable inputs (pesticides and fertilisers) that damage the environment or harm the health of farmers and consumers. And it makes better use of the knowledge and skills of farmers, so improving their self-reliance and capacities.[2]

The University of Essex has put together a database, which (by 2001) contained 208 examples of sustainable agriculture initiatives in 52 developing countries. These initiatives show that significant improvements in agricultural production and food security can be achieved through the use of regenerative technologies and the full participation of farmers in the processes of planning, research and extension. Some of the initiatives were long established; in others, farmers had switched to using techniques that were more sustainable. Importantly, the survey shows that the biggest increases in food output are occurring in the poorest farming sector.[3]

In many of the initiatives analysed, crop yields have more than doubled compared with the period before the adoption of sustainable agriculture. For non-irrigated crops, yields typically increased by 50 to 100 per cent and by even more in some cases. For 146,000 farmers cultivating roots – potato, sweet potato and cassava – average food production increased by 150 per cent. For irrigated crops, the gains were much smaller: 5 to 10 per cent. Livestock productivity was also found to increase, along with meat and milk production.

Some of the initiatives can be classified as organic or semi-organic, others as low external-input agriculture (see pp. 43–51), while some go further into the category of permaculture. It is clear that low external-input agriculture does not necessarily mean low-output agriculture, but that it can, on the contrary, be highly productive.

PERMACULTURE

The purest form of low external-input agriculture is permaculture which, strictly speaking, makes no use of inputs from outside a farm's immediate locality, not even manure or credit facilities. Permaculture spread rapidly in the last two decades of the twentieth century and is often proving highly productive in terms of overall farm output. The word 'permaculture' was coined by Australian, Bill Mollison, in the late 1970s. At its most basic, the word is an abbreviation of permanent agriculture. Mollison defines permaculture as 'the conscious design and maintenance of agriculturally productive ecosystems, which have the diversity, stability and resilience of natural ecosystems'.[4] Permaculture can be practised in rural and urban areas, and can be either subsistence farming or market-oriented. The practice is knowledge intensive and there are now permaculture institutes in most developing countries.[5]

Permaculture is doubly organic because its emphasis on 'recycling' makes sure that nutrients continue to revolve to the benefit of a farm. It is more 'energy conscious' than normal organic farming; its practitioners look wider than agriculture and recognise that energy is a scarce commodity.

While permaculture systems vary, they usually involve the careful mix of trees and crops to obtain maximum yields, the use of mulches, the integration of livestock and crops, and the use of green manures (ground cover plants) to protect soil and build up soil fertility. Tree crops are used for fodder as well as for controlling soil erosion. Plants which are drought-tolerant, like mulberry, may be planted on the least productive areas of farms. Practitioner Mike Feingold states:

> Permaculture is about making sure there's diversity so that risks are being spread, not all eggs are in one basket. It's about making sure that systems are integrated, self-regulated, and that each part of a system has a range of different functions. And it's about making sure that systems are efficient in terms of their use of energy. It's about good use of resources, about using local resources to meet local needs; permaculture is about the integration of what is grown in the land to the local economy.[6]

Food output rises spectacularly when farmers switch to permaculture. Farmers who convert from chemical farming may experience an initial drop in output (not always, however; see section on Nepal below), but increases of 300 to 400 per cent, and even higher, can eventually result. Some farmers convert to permaculture over a five-year period, converting a fifth of their land each year, gradually introducing different crops and reducing their inputs of chemicals to the point where they eventually eliminate them.

Permaculture is strong in parts of Africa, including Zimbabwe and Botswana, and in countries such as India and Mexico, Nepal, China and Vietnam, also in tropical South America. It has spread in marginal and degraded land – in Nepal, for example – on the terrace rises, the least productive areas, enabling many farmers to develop their most marginal land.

Because permaculture has often been implemented by people with few resources, they have tested and developed ideas and programmes using local materials skills.

EVIDENCE FROM AFRICA, ASIA AND LATIN AMERICA

There is now considerable evidence that substantial growth in agricultural output is possible, even in degraded land areas, whilst at the same time protecting and, moreover, regenerating natural resources. The evidence shows that regenerative and low-input agriculture can be highly productive. It explodes the myth that chemical fertiliser is needed to feed the world. Case studies also show that success is more likely when farmers participate fully in new initiatives.

The following are some of the initiatives that come under sustainable agriculture/organic agriculture/permaculture initiative.

New way for rice

When small farmers in Madagascar employed a new way of growing rice in the late 1980s, the results were so startling that agricultural scientists could hardly believe they were possible. Yields of around two tonnes per hectare shot up to around 8 to 10 tonnes per hectare, without either chemical fertilisers, pesticides or expensive seed varieties, and by breaking some of the conventional 'rules' of rice management. For years the new technique, known as the System of Rice Intensification (SRI), was virtually ignored.

The system was developed in Madagascar by an agronomist priest, Henri de Laudanié, working with a small farmers' group, Association Tefy Saina. Traditionally, rice is transplanted into fields at around eight weeks when it seems the plant is strong and likely to survive, and three or more seedlings are planted in clumps in the hope that one will fully mature. But with SRI, seedlings are transplanted at around six days and planted individually, enabling farmers to use less seed.

For thousands of years lowland rice has been grown under flooded conditions to ensure water supply and reduced weed problems. But while rice can survive in water, it is not an aquatic plant. Farmers in Madagascar noted that root growth was far greater if the plant was not kept continually submerged in water. 'The plants receive more oxygen and nutrients from the atmosphere and derive greater benefit from the warmth of the sun', said Sebastién Rafaralahy of Association Tefy Saina.[7] Using the SRI system the soil is kept continually wet only during the reproductive stage when the plant is producing grains. During the rest of the growth cycle the rice fields are irrigated in the evening and dry during the day.

Using their own seed, some 20,000 farmers have now adopted the method in Madagascar and yields have proved to be sustainable. After being evaluated by Cornell University in the United States, the system has spread to other countries, including major rice growers such as Bangladesh, China and Indonesia. In China yields of 9 to 10.5 tonnes per hectare were achieved in the first year of the system, compared with the national average of 6 tonnes per hectare.

Sustainable agriculture in Ethiopia

The Cheha Integrated Rural Development Project has been working in south-west Ethiopia since the severe drought of 1984. It has promoted organic manures for soil fertility, introduced new varieties of crops (vegetables) and trees (fruit and forest) and also veterinary services.

Some 12,500 farm households have adopted sustainable agriculture on about 5000 hectares, resulting in a 70 per cent improvement of overall nutrition levels within the project area, along with a 60 per cent increase in crop yields. Some farmers have begun to produce excess crops which they sell in local markets, earning much needed income for their families. Thus an area once reliant on emergency food aid has now become able to feed itself and have enough left over to contribute to surplus.[8]

Zai holes

Zai holes are an adaptation of a traditional farming technique that makes use of termites to improve soil fertility and increase crop yields. A hole is dug in the dry season – 20 cm by 20 cm by 10 cm deep, although it can be larger – and filled with mulch such as crop residues or manures. This leads to increased termite activity, which in turn increases the rate of water infiltration when the rain falls. The holes are planted with millet or sorghum and also help to protect seedlings from wind damage. In one area of West Africa, where millet yields were often less than 350 kg per hectare, the digging of Zai holes transformed the situation: yields soared to between 1000 to 2000 kg per hectare.[9]

Zai holes can be combined with other low-cost techniques to further increase yields. Under the Project Agro-Forestier (PAF) in Burkina Faso (an Oxfam initiative), a device has been developed that enables farmers to trace the contours for laying out bunds (embankments). After two years of joint experimentation, locally adapted versions of contour rock bunds, combined with crop planting in Zai holes filled with mulch, improved crop yields and proved effective at harvesting water. Increased termite activity increases the water penetration when the rains come. Yields have improved by some 40 per cent on treated land and hold up well in low rainfall years.

Deep dig rejuvenation

Deep dig rejuvenation is a kind of 'layer composting', which involves digging a 2 foot deep pit, putting the soil on one side, and then adding layers of organic fertiliser material. Green leaves, split banana trunks, compost or raw cow manure are put into the pit, ashes and mustard-seed pomace are then added; the ashes kill any cutworm eggs that are present in the cowdung. This is churned up as much as possible and a 3 inch layer of stone and weed-free soil is spread over the area; the layering is then repeated. After this second layer, the ground returns to its original level. The topsoil is then returned and more compost and ashes added if necessary. Farmers in Nepal, where the technique appears to have originated, have enjoyed a fourfold increase in crop yields.[10]

Organic farming in India

Gloria Land Farm in Pondicherry, India, has put organic farming into practice and is making it pay through diversified cropping patterns and methods to induce soil fertility. Run by Julie and Vivek Cariappa, the farm cultivates banana, paddy, grass, mango, coconut, lime and gooseberry simultaneously. Cotton, rice, millet, sugar cane and vegetables are also grown. 'Even if one crop fails, the others provide returns. And if one crop absorbs more soil nutrients, the others compensate by fixing nitrogen', says Julie Cariappa.

The farm uses plant-based fertilisers and pesticides: neem (margosa) leaves, plants and weeds that grow in the fallow fields, cow dung and crop residues to restore soil fertility; biogas slurry, weeds, marigold and dung as compost; and plant-based pesticides and cattle urine for controlling pests. The Cariappas also use innovative pesticide techniques, such as spraying a mixture of garlic juice and water on cabbage patches and spreading dried cowdung soaked in water for a day on vegetable crops to keep away pests and enhance productivity. 'In organic farming, we don't have rigid formulas for applying inputs', says Julie Cariappa; 'everything, from sowing to harvesting, is experimented with and many things learned on the job. It is not preplanned and unlike scientists, farmers don't have to depend on outsiders. Yields are favourable when compared with farms that use synthetic fertilisers and pesticides, and returns are good'.[11]

Nepal: maintaining output with new techniques

It is a commonly held belief that in switching from high- to low-external input, or chemical to organic farming systems, a drop in yield is to be expected for a period. In a country such as Nepal, where over 90 per cent of the population is dependent on agriculture as a primary source of livelihood, this is clearly an unacceptable situation. There are no grants, subsidies or set-aside to bide farmers over the lean periods.[12]

Permaculture was first introduced to Nepal in 1986, where the largest permaculture-based initiative is in the hills of Western Nepal – the Jajarkot Permaculture Programme (JPP). This was set up in 1988, initially on an acre of land. From here it has spread to over fifty villages, employing some 120 staff, mainly farmers from local villages in its working areas, and with over 12,000 members.

The JPP found that the technologies it introduced and taught to farmers were taken up and often modified and improved by farmers themselves. 'The programme had to relearn these technologies and approaches in an information-cycle that continuously feeds back and strives to improve itself, providing a better service to user groups', says Chris Evans, the programme's technical advisor.

The JPP developed demonstration sites to show how sustainable agriculture can be practised when correct design of farms, together with social programmes, is implemented. Integration of trees, use of all areas of farm land, improvement and utilisation of common property resources, and the use of other techniques, such as beekeeping, provided the resources that were needed to increase crop yields without clearing new land.

Results are impressive. At one demonstration farm a 50 per cent increase in paddy production – to 3,600 kg/ha – was achieved over three years by using green manures. Local farmers, who had been suffering from decreasing yields – 2,000 kg/ha – and increasing costs, began to follow the example of the successful farm. Another farmer tried using sorghum as a green manure, ploughing it in after a month's growth and prior to planting potatoes. He claimed this led to a 300 per cent increase in potato yield. One JPP resource centre reported a 400 per cent increase in wheat yield.

The above examples of increased production were all attained without a drop in yield, which, Chris Evans asserts,

is the only way of demonstrating appropriate improvements. This emphasises the application of the 'rolling permaculture' approach whereby new systems are introduced alongside traditional ones, and are designed to enhance and diversify production rather than replace it. Where design is applied to degraded or fallow sites – eroded slopes, bare land, etc. – then there is more imposition of a total design rather than the rolling approach, but such sites are not in production anyway, so cannot suffer the 'dip' effect either. The JPP's results to date are so encouraging that part of its work is to apply and teach models of sustainable development, including sustainable agriculture and permaculture, on a national and even international scale.[13]

Thailand: another success story

In some developing countries focused rural development strategies are an effective part of the new green revolution. Thailand's successful fight against food insecurity is described in an FAO report, for example, as a model for long-term community-based action programmes. The incidence of poverty and malnutrition has fallen dramatically in Thailand in the last two decades, thanks to a poverty alleviation strategy focused on reducing malnutrition and supporting sustainable rural development. As a result, the percentage of people living in poverty fell from 32.6 per cent in 1988 to 11.4 per cent in 1996 and severe malnutrition amongst young children was eliminated.[14]

Output rises in Brazil's Santa Catarina

The state government extension and research service, EPAGRI, works with farmers in the Southern Brazilian state of Santa Catarina. The technological focus is on soil and water conservation at the microwatershed level using contour grass barriers, contour ploughing and green manures.

Some 60 cover-crop species have been tested with farmers, including leguminous plants such as velvetbean, jackbean, lablab, cowpeas, vetches and crotalarias, and non-legumes such as oats and turnips. For the farmers, no cash was involved other than the purchase of seed. Seed is planted during fallow periods and used in the cropping system with varieties such as maize, onions, cassava, wheat, grapes, tomatoes and soybean.

The major on-farm impact of the project has been on crop yields, soil quality and moisture retention, and labour demand. Maize yields have risen since 1987 from 3 to 5 t/ha [tonnes per hectare] and soybeans from 2.8 to 4.7 t/ha. Soils are darker in colour, moist and biologically active.

The reduced need for most weeding and ploughing has meant significant labour savings for small farmers.[15]

Permaculture in Ecuador

Based in Ecuador, Permacultura America Latina (PAL) was created to teach and spread permaculture throughout South America. It was pioneered by Australian, Gavin Tinning, who worked there for five years to create a humid tropics demonstration farm.

The farm, the Madre Selva Permaculture Farm, is located in the mangroves of the Pacific Coast. Mulched out of abysmally poor soils, it is now a demonstration site that provides a resource base supporting a myriad of satellite projects. PAL has run a number of design courses and graduates have established their own projects. One is a Quichua community which has built massive swales and reforested its denuded ancestral mountain in the Cotopaxi Province.

Two of the courses were held on behalf of the indigenous Shipibo who live in the area of Pucallpa, close to the Peruvian/Brazilian border. Having lived sustainably from a nomadic *chakra* system of agriculture, the Shipibo have now been settled and, unfamiliar with physical permanence, have almost destroyed their soil base. Masterful fishermen, their protein base was the fabulously abundant fish variety of the ox-bow lakes of the Ucayali river. But with the pressure of urban population encroachment, the fish stocks are rapidly dwindling and the Shipibo face cultural annihilation.

Eight native species have so far been introduced and further examination is taking place. A nursery for forest food crops and fruit trees to feed the fish has been established. The project is a cutting-edge endeavour to relieve the Shipibo and present an Amazonian model for fish production. The hope is that the system will become an alternative to the continuing destruction of natural resources by governments.[16]

How Crops for Export Can Be Grown Organically: The Case of Ethiopian Coffee

Coffee originated in Ethiopia and is a central part of the economy. Some 700,000 small-scale farmers grow the crop, usually alongside food crops, and almost a quarter of the population depend on it for part of their livelihood. For many it is their only source of cash, the means of sending children to school, of paying for healthcare and buying basic consumer goods.

Ethiopia depends on exports of coffee for around 65 per cent of foreign earnings. With about 2.3 per cent of the global coffee market, it is Africa's third largest exporter of coffee (behind Ivory Coast and Uganda), exporting 2 million 60 kg bags in 2000.

Around 95 per cent of Ethiopia's coffee output is organic, grown without chemicals, fertilisers or pesticides. Pests and disease are controlled by traditional farming practices, including intercropping and the use of green mulches. These are prominent around the coffee trees. Ethiopian coffee is not, however, certified organic and neither government nor growers benefit from the higher prices that organic coffee commands. The country's Coffee and Tea Authority has developed an organic certification scheme, with help from the Swiss government, the International Coffee Organisation and the Amsterdam-based Common Fund for Commodities. The Geneva-based International Trade Centre is helping to set up a national certifier for organic coffee that will be internationally recognised.*

Such certification is difficult to obtain, however, and could be thwarted by chemical fertilisers applied to nearly all food crops. Ethiopia's Ministry of Agriculture seeks to persuade the country's farmers to use chemical fertilisers in potentially productive areas. As much of Ethiopia's coffee is intercropped, 'the use of chemicals on nearby crops will endanger organic certification', said an official of Agri Service Ethiopia, a voluntary organisation. **

Certified organic coffee holds out the prospect of an important boost to the earnings and livelihoods of Ethiopian smallholders who grow coffee. With organic foods and beverages increasingly in demand in Western countries, there is clear scope for growers of other export crops to convert to organic.

Sources: John Madeley, 'Times turn hard for Ethiopia's small-scale coffee growers', *Financial Times*, 30 March 2001; Conversation with author, March 2001.

CHAPTER 6

GETTING THE
TECHNOLOGIES RIGHT

For poor farmers, GM technology is not an option.
Miquel Altieri

THE INTERNATIONAL AGRICULTURAL
RESEARCH CENTRES

They are walled and gated and sealed off from the community around them. Inside these august institutions, earnest scientists conduct a range of agricultural research, trying to develop 'modern' technologies. When they finish work for the day most of them climb into their cars or walk to luxurious housing within the compound, a stark contrast to the poverty that lies on the other side of the wall.

These institutions – international agricultural research centres (IARCs) – all exist to do something about that poverty. But they stand accused of being 'too large, too inflexible, too expensive, insufficiently impact-orientated. Isolation – sometimes increased by arrogance – is the result'.[1]

The 16 centres – 13 of them in developing countries – are virtually a microcosm of the world as a whole; islands of affluence in a world of poverty. They make up a network that is coordinated by the Washington-based Consultative Group for International Agricultural Research (CGIAR). In 1999, the CGIAR and its 16 centres had a budget of US$349 million and employed about 8,600 people.

The money comes from 58 governments, private foundations and international and regional agencies. The World Bank, FAO and the United Nations Development Programme (UNDP) are co-sponsors.

Set up in the 1960s and 1970s the broad objective of the centres is to increase the quantity and improve the quality of food in the developing countries. While their expenditure is less than 4 per cent of the global expenditure on agricultural research, the centres have an influence out of all proportion to their size and budgets, and are seen as setting standards of professional excellence. 'Through their training of national scientists, their international networking of research programmes, their publications, and their prestige, the IARCs spread and sustain the dominant concepts, values, methods and behaviour of agricultural science'.[2]

A number of them were at the forefront of the 1960s' Green Revolution, the development of high-yielding rice and wheat varieties. Their rhetoric in the 1990s suggests that their focus is on poverty reduction: 'reducing poverty through cutting-edge science'.[3] The substance amounts to less than the rhetoric, however, and now the centres are moving into the genetic modification of crops, which could spell ruin for small-farmer agriculture.

The CGIAR centres operate in largely English-speaking countries, although a number are in Latin America. Only one, a rice institute, is based in a French-speaking country, Côte d'Ivoire. The French government has its own agricultural research network, CIRAD (Centre de coopération internationale en recherche agronomique et développement) which spends around US$175 million a year. While there is some sharing of ideas, the two networks operate largely independently of each other.

The chief criticisms of the IARCs is that their technology is not sufficiently focused on helping people who are hungry, that the 1960s high-technology Green Revolution has helped larger and better endowed rather than poorer farmers, and that their claim to be helping to reduce poverty is weak. Also that their research concentrates on higher value crops, such as rice, rather than the crops of the poor, such as pulses and coarser grains. And some have attracted criticism because of their eagerness to embrace GM technology.

The case for

In an address to a workshop in September 1999, entitled 'How does research reduce poverty', an official of the International Centre for Tropical Agriculture (CIAT) appeared to speak for all the IARCs:

> Research improves farm income by offering technological innovations that boost agricultural productivity. Strong evidence points to massive productivity increases during recent decades in impoverished areas. The best-known examples are the widespread adoption of modern rice and wheat varieties. But other cases include virus-free sweet potatoes for poor farmers in hillside areas of China, livestock technologies in Sub-Saharan Africa, and new cassava varieties in Nigeria. Though small farmers sometimes adopt new technologies more slowly than large producers, large numbers of small farmers have adopted and benefited … Far from locking rural people into poverty on small farms, agricultural research has helped many of them find an exit.
>
> Research has also benefited landless workers through job creation in a more productive agriculture. Many farm labourers have migrated to more favoured regions where farmers have taken up new varieties. One of the greatest benefits of agricultural research in developing countries, it is claimed, has been cheaper food made possible by more efficient crop production. This has especially helped the poor, as they spend much of their income on food.
>
> The rural poor pursue different 'pathways out of poverty', and research helps these people find a way forward. In many households, agricultural production is frequently the responsibility of women, who benefit from innovations in the production of staple foods and from labour-saving devices. Many research organisations have given high priority to crops that are grown and consumed mainly by the poor, and they have targeted regions where large numbers of poor people live. Yet, empirical evidence suggests that this research has not always registered high gains in reducing poverty. The prospects for continued impact from agricultural research on the food security, poverty, and environmental fronts have never been better. CGIAR centres, together with their research partners, have accumulated a huge stock of 'social capital' in the form of networks and other partnerships.
>
> Critics claim that many poor people have not received their fair share of the research benefits and that some of these have actually gone to the rich. Such criticisms should serve agricultural researchers as a constant reminder that their work can be better targeted and better managed. The shortcomings of research should not divert attention from the impressive record of success.[4]

Some concrete achievements

Between 1985 and 2000 I visited most of the IARCs and found that they vary enormously. Some of them are doing valuable work, using chemical-free methods and conventional breeding techniques. Some are helping the poor with ideas such as integrated pest management. Others were much less impressive.

One of the most impressive, and possibly the one most geared to helping the poorest farmers, is the International Crops Research Institute for the Semi-Arid Tropics (ICRISAT), based in Patancheru in the Indian state of Hyderabad. The centre researches into 'orphan' crops such as pigeonpea, groundnut and pearl millet — known as orphan because they have been largely neglected in agricultural research. ICRISAT has developed a low-cost biological insecticide to combat a pest that threatens pigeonpea, for example, a nutritious crop grown mostly by small-scale farming families for their own use. It has worked with the New Delhi-based Indian Council of Agricultural Research to develop new varieties that thrive in rainfed conditions. Its research into the coarse-grain pearl millet has also proved valuable.

The International Institute of Tropical Agriculture (IITA) in Nigeria, CIAT in Colombia, and the International Centre for Agricultural Research in Dry Areas (ICARDA) in Syria have also developed low-cost technologies to help small-scale farmers, which do not require chemicals. At the International Maize and Wheat Improvement Center (CIMMYT) new breeds of tropical maize have been developed which can increase harvests by 40 per cent in difficult environments such as heat and drought. Researchers have been able to modify wheat, once mostly restricted to temperate and subtropical zones, to make it productive even in hot climates.

There is nonetheless a high-tech approach at some of the centres which is not necessarily relevant to advancing food security. Often there are contradictions. While scientists at a centre may be working on ways of tackling problems that require the application of fewer chemicals, people at the same institute appear unable to envisage an agricultural system that does not depend on such inputs.

IRRI – a more controversial case

One of the earliest and largest of the centres is also one of the most controversial: the Manila-based International Rice Research Institute (IRRI) which was at the forefront of developing new strains of rice in the 1960s. IRRI claims that an independent study of the impact of improved rice varieties and other crops has found that, over the past 40 years, these crops have significantly reduced prices for poor consumers, saved thousands of hectares of forests from being turned into farmland, and reduced the number of malnourished children.

Were it not for the development of improved varieties, rice prices for consumers could have been up to 41 per cent higher, claims IRRI, 'rice-producing nations would be importing up to 8 per cent more food ... and between 1.5 and 2 per cent more children would have been malnourished in developing countries. This seemingly small figure in percentage terms translates into millions of better-fed children in reality'.[5]

But critics in the Philippines see IRRI rather differently and have called for the centre to be closed down. They accuse it of being 'the bane of rice farmers in the Philippines. IRRI's costly inputs of chemicals and pesticides to grow rice have devastated the land and ruined the livelihoods of farmers'.[6] This seems to be borne out by a Philippine Rice Research Institute study which found that 48 of the Philippines' 54 provinces have depleted soils. Also, the conditions under which Asian rice growers farm are very different from the large and sophisticated plots at IRRI where experiments are conducted. And critics point out that IRRI's Annual Reports, from 1983 to 1999, show that the centre received grants from chemical companies such as Ciba-Geigy, Monsanto, Shell and Union Carbide.[7]

What strikes a visitor to IRRI's test plots near Manila is that all the tests seem to be conducted on the basis that applications of chemical fertiliser are essential. Organically grown rice seems to have little or no place in IRRI's thinking. Even for the poorest farmers, the use of chemical fertiliser 'is seen as the way forward.[8] By its neglect of organic methods of rice production IRRI is not helping the small-scale farmer who cannot afford fertiliser.

Some IRRI scientists are engaged on research that is helping the small farmer. They have encouraged integrated pest management, for example, and shown that rice farmers can reduce their applications of pesticide without yields being affected. This cuts the cost to farmers and increases their overall returns.[9] But IRRI's embracing of genetically modified (GM) technology is again attracting criticism (see pp. 59–64).

There is a clear need for the centres to undertake 'better targeted and better managed' research. With all their skilled people and funds, the centres have not made the impact they could have made on developing crops for the poor that could eliminate hunger. Research at the centres is relatively high cost and sometimes outmatched by the voluntary sector at much lower cost. As the example of rice in Madagascar in the last chapter showed, it was a voluntary organisation that developed ways of significantly increasing rice yields.

In some cases the centres have failed to improve on crops developed many years ago. A variety of winter barley 'Unumli-Arpa', for example, developed over 50 years at a research institute started by Russian scientist Nikolai Vavilov, has been cultivated in Central Asia for about half a century and is still one of the best in terms of its heat- and drought-resistance in rainfed conditions.[10]

Three criticisms

The centres therefore have some way to go. 'The centralised technology transfer approach practised and propagated by the CG [Consultative Group] centres, rhetoric notwithstanding, has tended to be insensitive to local contexts and to the needs and interests of their poorer clients'.[11] There is a danger that IARCs, with their greater prestige, will pass on an inappropriate culture of behaviour and attitudes, and even stifle national or local participatory initiatives.

The CGIAR system needs to put right three serious weaknesses in its network.

- *The needs of small farmers* Nowhere in the system is research focused on the special problems of small-farm agriculture. Centres individually address part of the problems but with limited wider application. The result is that the system generally does not

INTERNATIONAL AGRICULTURAL RESEARCH CENTRES

The Consultative Group on International Agricultural Research (CGIAR) is 'a worldwide network of research centres supported by an international donor group'. The centres are:

Centre for International Forestry Research (CIFOR), Jakarta, Indonesia
International Centre for Agricultural Research in Dry Areas (ICARDA), Aleppo, Syria
International Centre for Living Aquatic Resource Management (ICLARM), Manila, Philippines
International Centre for Research in Agroforestry (ICRAF), Nairobi, Kenya
International Centre for Tropical Agriculture (CIAT), Cali, Colombia
International Crops Research Institute for the Semi-Arid Tropics (ICRISAT), Patancheru, India
International Food Policy Research Institute (IFPRI), Washington DC, USA
International Institute of Tropical Agriculture (IITA), Ibadan, Nigeria
International Irrigation Management Institute (IIMI), Colombo, Sri Lanka
International Livestock Research Institute (ILRI), Nairobi, Kenya.
International Maize and Wheat Improvement Centre (CIMMYT), Mexico
International Plant Genetic Resources Institute (IPGRI), Rome, Italy
International Potato Centre (CIP), Lima, Peru
International Rice Research Institute (IRRI), Manila, Philippines
International Service for National Agricultural Research (ISNAR), The Hague, The Netherlands
West African Rice Development Association (WARDA), Bouaké 01, Côte d'Ivoire.

In 1998 the centres created a charitable and educational organisation called 'Future Harvest', which aims to 'advance debate and catalyse action for a world with less poverty, a healthier human family, and a better environment'.

provide integrated advice on the whole range of crop, livestock and other economic components of small farming. 'Given the problems of small farmers, highlighted by the widespread abandonment of small farms and the move to megacities, a strong argument can be made for a new institute to emphasise the interests of small farmers in developing countries'.[12]

APPROPRIATE RESEARCH

'Appropriately focused agricultural research' has helped to reduce undernourishment 'substantially in a number of countries', claims the FAO's *State of Food Insecurity in the World Report*. It cites Ghana where farmers were able to exploit new market opportunities for cassava, thanks to an aggressive cassava research and market promotion programme based on high-yielding varieties which had to be adapted to local climatic and soil conditions. Between 1990 and 1998, annual consumption of cassava in Ghana increased from 126 kg to 232 kg per capita.

Source: FAO, *State of Food Insecurity in the World Report*, 2000.

- *Low external-input farming*   Again, nowhere in the system is research focused on organic, or even on low external-input farming. Yet these are the types of agriculture that are practised by the vast majority of the world's small-scale farmers. Again there is a strong argument for a new institute that focuses on organic and semi-organic agriculture.
- *Genetic modification*   But the biggest weakness of the CG system lies in its attitude to genetic modification. In 1998 the CGIAR adopted a policy which recommended that the 16 centres do not use terminator technology − a GM technology designed to stop seed germination − in their crop improvement programmes. Breeders would have their hands tied by such technology so it clearly does not suit them. Some centres, however, including for example the Washington-based IFPRI, are embracing and advocating the use of other GM technologies. Such advocacy could have serious consequences for small-scale farmers and for food security.

GM TECHNOLOGY

Genetically modified crop technology involves the insertion of an alien gene into a plant to give it certain traits, for example vitamin enrichment and drought tolerance. The gene may come from a different kind of plant, from an animal, a virus or a bacterium. In crop breeding terms the introduction of such genes is unnatural and the effects unknown. It bypasses conventional breeding and brings about combinations of genes that would not occur naturally. 'You are adding complications into the natural system. If you make a mistake with GM technology, you could ruin your genetic base', warns Ethiopian scientist Tewolde Gebre Egziabher.[13]

To make a contribution to food security, GM crops would have to prove they are safe to people and the environment, that they do not damage the livelihoods of small-scale farmers and that these farmers could have cheap and ready access to the technology. This could take a long time as there are still many unknown factors. 'Genetic engineering is designed to transfer genes horizontally between species that do not interbreed', says Mae-Wan Ho. No one knows the risks to people's health of doing this. 'The insertion of foreign genes into the host genome has long been known to have many harmful and fatal effects, including cancer'.[14]

On the environment, the risks are considerable. Once GM crops are introduced into the environment they are there to stay. They allow for no second chances. There is a real danger of GM pollution, with the traits of GM crops spreading to crops in neighbouring fields, an unwelcome 'colonisation' of another's field.

Many GM crops are made to resist herbicides. But herbicide applications could kill everything else, apart from the GM crop, including beneficial insects such as ladybirds and also important medicines and herbs. Should GM seeds spread, more herbicide would have to be applied and weeds in nearby fields could develop resistance to the poison. Such 'superweeds' would require higher doses of herbicide. Applications of pesticide will not necessarily be reduced with GM crops. Recent trials of GM cotton in India showed there was little difference in the amount of pesticide that had to be sprayed on GM and conventional cotton.

The widespread adoption of GM crops would also mean the spread of monocropping and threaten further loss of plant genetic diversity – the very basis of food security. To those who seek to protect plant genetic diversity, including the CGIAR centres, this should be of considerable concern.

There is little sign that companies involved in GM technology are interested in raising yields of basic foodcrops. 'Most GM technology has not been developed with Third World needs in mind. Rather, these techniques were developed primarily for large-scale agriculture in the industrialised world'.[15] Even if the companies become interested, the timescale is lengthy. 'If we ever find that GM technology would bring us major benefits in years to come, then let's look at it. But you have to wait as long as it takes to sort out the problems – a few generations, perhaps a hundred years. We are tampering with the foundations of life. We must wait long enough – or face the consequences', says Dr. Tewolde.[16] GM crops seem unlikely to make a contribution to reducing hunger in the twenty-first century, let alone by 2015.

GM coffee – what consequences?

Advocates of GM technology hope that it will eventually raise food output. But should the technology lead to higher yields of crops grown for export, this would lower world prices and have serious consequences for smallholders who grow such crops for income. In February 1999, for example, the University of Hawaii was granted a US patent on GM coffee, based on using the chemical ethylene to encourage the ripening of coffee cherries. The cherries from GM coffee can only ripen when sprayed with ethylene.[17]

A Hawaiian-based company, Integrated Coffee Technologies Inc. (ICTI), was set up to commercialise the GM coffee. 'They [the growers] are going to be able to increase their yields and decrease their labour ... labour will be decreased by perhaps 50 per cent', claims John Stiles of ICTI.[18] The technology will help larger farmers and plantation owners to increase their profits by employing fewer people and is intended to increase yields in mechanised harvested crops.

Should GM coffee be commercialised successfully, then world coffee output would increase still further, and prices fall even lower. For small-scale coffee growers this could be a disaster; they would have little hope of growing coffee profitably. The balance between supply and demand would be further tipped against them. Many coffee growers are facing destitution even without further falls that could be induced by GM coffee (see Chapter 3).

GM coffee, if it ever came to fruition, would fundamentally change the nature of coffee growing. Most small-scale farmers would cease to grow the crop. Most coffee would be grown on plantations with heavy applications of chemical fertilisers and pesticides – notably herbicides for weed control, insecticides to ward off insect pests and fungicides to control disease.

Golden rice

In certain cases GM technology could contribute to helping over-come specific problems such as blindness caused by Vitamin A deficiency (VAD). Even this is highly controversial and it is arguable whether GM technology is needed to this end. 'Substantial progress has been made towards the elimination of VAD', according to the World Health Organisation.[19]

The most substantial development with GM technology has come from IRRI, over a GM rice, so-called Golden Rice, designed to help tackle VAD. In January 2001, IRRI, the Rockefeller Foundation and the transnational corporation (TNC) Syngenta (see Chapter 12) announced that the first research samples of pro-Vitamin A en-riched Golden Rice had arrived in Asia. 'Golden Rice', they said, was a 'genetically modified rice which contains beta-carotene and other carotenoids ... IRRI scientists will now begin work that will play a key role in an international effort to further investigate the safety and utility of Golden Rice in combating VAD which is re-sponsible for 500,000 cases of irreversible blindness and 1–2 million deaths worldwide each year'.[20] The delivery of Golden Rice from the inventors' laboratories in Europe was possible as a result of the dona-tion of intellectual property licences from Syngenta, Bayer, Monsanto, Orynova, and Zeneca Mogen, said IRRI.

However, within weeks of the announcement, the Rockefeller Foundation, which funded the research, was backtracking. The project, which has been used worldwide by supporters of GM crops as a justification for the technology, appears likely to generate only a fraction of the additional Vitamin A it promised. A Rockefeller Foundation spokesperson is quoted as saying: 'We do not consider Golden Rice to be the solution to the Vitamin A deficiency problem ... the public relations uses of Golden Rice have gone too far'.[21]

According to an inter-NGO agency report 'evidence shows that Golden Rice will have little effect on reducing VAD, providing at most 20 per cent of an adult's Vitamin A requirements'.[22] It is difficult to see Golden Rice as anything other than an attempt by agribusiness and IRRI to win 'respectability' for a GM technology, as 'a foot-in-the-door' to try to gain wider acceptance. It could also deflect attention away from alternatives. 'The best chance in fighting VAD is to better use the inexpensive and nutritious foods already available'.[23]

The fundamental issues

In theory GM technology could make a contribution in helping to develop crops that, for example, have resistance to drought, heat and cold, and which are virus resistant. In practice it puts 'too much power over food into too few hands'.[24] Through the patent system GM crops hand power over the food chain to TNCs. To have a future, GM technology would have to prove that it is safe for people and the environment, that higher yields of food crops would result and hungry people benefit, and that it could be controlled by small-scale farmers rather than by large corporations. Given the patent system, this seems unlikely.

The fundamental issue is control. 'Monopolistic control illustrates how a handful of TNCs are using intellectual property as a powerful market tool to stifle innovation, shackle public sector research and foster ever-increasing industry consolidation'.[25]

Corporations show no signs of letting go of the patents they hold on the seeds. On the contrary, Monsanto has applied for patents on its Terminator Technology – seeds which self-destruct after one season – in over 70 countries. Seed is a particularly sensitive issue for small-scale farmers. 'Seed is a farmer's dignity; without seed, a farmer is a potential migrant', says Saley Younissi, a farmer in Tera, Niger. As long as TNCs enforce their patent rights, control of GM technology cannot pass to the farmer. GM mega-businesses could be particularly damaging in developing countries, dominating the market, taking out patents on farmer seed and even making it difficult for farmers to save and exchange their own seed.

GM advocates claim that developing countries need the technology, although there is little evidence of higher yields from GM crops. Conventional varieties of soya are still mostly outperforming GM varieties in the US, according to research, for example, at the University of Wisconsin. Africans have made clear their opposition. At a meeting of the FAO's Commission on Genetic Resources, 24 delegates of African governments issued a strongly worded statement saying that GM technologies 'will destroy the diversity, local knowledge and sustainable agricultural systems that our farmers have developed for millennia, and thus undermine our capacity to feed ourselves'.[26]

Because of corporate control over the food chain, GM technology could worsen rather than improve prospects for hungry people. It could be a death knell for millions of small farmers who could see their farms taken over and turned into large units, growing crops for export while indigenous populations go hungry. Only if they have control over the technology are GM crops likely to help farmers to reduce the poverty that keeps them hungry.

GM crops are being pushed by agro–industry because they are 'marketable'. Sustainable low-cost solutions are outside that category and are therefore of no interest to the industry. But even people in industry have owned up to GM's limitations. 'If anyone tells you that GM is going to feed the world, tell them that it is not … to feed the world takes political and financial will – it's not about production and distribution', said a director of Novartis, one of the world's largest biotechnology companies.[27] Only the final word of this sentence would be open to qualification.

It is not credible for agribusiness to present GM crops as the saviour of the world's hungry. Overemphasis on the technology has clear dangers. It can divert attention away from the need to fund and encourage sustainable systems that can feed the world in a way that will halve world hunger by 2015.

The attention and research going to GM crops means a neglect of the food crops and agriculture of interest to the poor. The United Nations Development Programme, which promoted GM crops in its latest Human Development Report, 'has reduced its support for traditional agriculture', alleges Von Henandez of Greenpeace Southeast Asia. GM technology further undermines biodiversity, which is the key to keeping on top of crop diseases and vital for crop breeding, for work at the IARCs, for food security itself. Science can take wrong turnings; agricultural research needs to be re-oriented to concentrate on the crops of smallholders.

GM 'WILL NOT FEED THE HUNGRY'

Genetically modified crops 'will not feed the hungry, they will make them poorer', says Hans Herren, Director-general of the International Centre of Insect Physiology and Ecology in Nairobi. The narrow base of these crops is against them, he believes, and their adoption would cause the further loss of diverse plant species which scientists need. 'Too narrow an approach to food security issues is dangerous. Africa needs a broad range of ecologically suited crop varieties. The concept of genetically modified crops is based on profit for seed and agrochemical companies, not the welfare of farmers'.

The solution lies not with GM crops, but with a 'different approach that enables farmers to have necessary credit facilities and manageable solutions to their agronomic problems. The problem is the lack of policies and will at government level to put agriculture at the top of the agenda. GM crops won't change that. In some instances, GM crops may be of use in increasing the quality of food crop varieties, but this is only relevant once abundance has been achieved ... I do not see the likelihood of GM crops making an impact on food production in Africa within the next 15 to 20 years'.

Source: Hans Herren, Speech to the Overseas Development Institute, London, October 1998.

CHAPTER 7

THE WATER SPRING

The skies are planted with water.

Kenyan farmer

Crops cannot grow, agriculture cannot thrive without water. Whether it comes from rivers, lakes, underground aquifers or from the sky, water is essential to farming. The availability of water gives impoverished farmers the potential to increase food output. For millions, however, water is a scarce resource and the lack if it is a big constraint to producing more food. In many water-scarce countries there are competing demands for water – households, industry, hotels all need it, but so too does agriculture. A key question is whether these demands can be reconciled. For food security the question is whether increasingly scarce water resources can be managed and organised to enable farmers to produce the food that is needed.

HOW MUCH IS THERE?

Of the earth's 1,360 million cubic kilometres of water, 97 per cent is in the oceans. Three-quarters of the freshwater is in glaciers and icebergs, another fifth is groundwater and less than 1 per cent is in lakes and rivers. Almost two-thirds of the renewable freshwater provided by annual rainfall over land evaporates. Given current global water use of 4,000 cubic kilometres, the remaining 14,000 cubic kilometres of effective runoff water would be adequate to meet demand for the foreseeable future if supplies were distributed equally across the world's population. But freshwater is distributed very unevenly across countries and regions within countries.

Water scarcity is increasing in many parts of the world. Some 30 countries are now 'water stressed', of which 20 are absolutely water scarce, according to the UN Food and Agriculture Organisation (FAO). By 2020, the number of water-scarce countries is likely to approach 35.[1] Virtually all developing countries, even those with adequate water overall, suffer from severe seasonal and regional shortages.

Water analysts use the following guide to identify when water scarcity becomes a serious problem: countries with freshwater resources of 1,000 to 1,600 cubic metres per capita per year face water stress, with major problems occurring in drought years. Countries are considered water scarce when annual internal renewable water resources are less than 1,000 cubic metres per capita per year.

Agriculture typically uses around 80 per cent of a country's water supplies. But most crop land in developing countries is not irrigated. Of cultivated land in Asia, 37 per cent is irrigated, in North Africa 24 per cent, in Latin America, 15 per cent. In Sub-Saharan Africa only 4 per cent of cultivated land is irrigated and three-quarters of this is in 6 countries. These figures refer to irrigation 'and do not include the many and diverse techniques of water harvesting and exploitation of residual moisture'.[2]

IRRIGATION: BIG DAMS AND LITTLE DAMS

Water for irrigating crops comes mainly from rivers and lakes, also from the sky. When water comes from rivers and lakes, an infrastructure is needed to bring it to the fields. Tapping rivers and lakes for irrigation has proved hugely controversial, chiefly because of the large-scale technology that has often been employed.

Big dams: the problems

Big dam schemes were an icon of the twentieth century – 45,000 big dams were constructed, more than one a day. The Tennessee Valley Dam became a United States showpiece of the 1930s; Egypt's

Aswan Dam was a showpiece of the 1950s. Today nearly half the world's rivers have a large dam.

Officially defined as dams more than 15 metres high, large dams were seen as one of the world's great technologies. Dam a river in a big way, allow the power of the trapped water to generate electricity, organise the water so that it irrigates land and helps to produce more food, the logic seems impeccable – both electricity and irrigation, at a stroke. But it's a stroke that has often proved fatal. In the twenty-first century there is a huge question mark over whether large dams should ever be built again.

Despite the millions of dollars sunk into them, these dams have often proved disastrous. Costs have been far higher than expected, environmental side-effects have been severe, millions of people have been dislocated, and the schemes have proved unsustainable. In a damning comment on such schemes in India, the country's former Prime Minister Rajiv Gandhi pointed out that of 246 large surface-irrigation projects that had started in India since 1951, only 65 were completed by 1986, and that little benefit had come from projects begun after 1970. 'For 16 years we have poured money out', he said, 'the people have got nothing back, no irrigation, no water, no increase in production, no help in their daily life'.[3]

This seems typical of the performance of large dams overall. In November 2000 the World Commission on Dams – an independent body set up in 1997 – published its findings. It said that large dams designed to deliver irrigation systems have 'typically fallen short of physical targets'.[4] In human terms perhaps the powerful statistic is that large dams have uprooted between 40 to 80 million people. Their homes and their land were flooded to make way for the new schemes and they were moved to other areas, often many miles away. The benefits of large dam schemes also tend to bypass the poor, who gain neither irrigation nor electricity. Millions of people 'living down-stream from the dams have also suffered serious harm to their livelihoods and the future productivity of their resources has been put at risk'.[5]

The Commission's report is doubtful about the future of large dams: 'The decision to build a large dam has been increasingly contested, to the point where the future of large dam building in many countries is in question'. The report's guidelines call for 'an open and participatory review of all on-going and planned projects'. Vulnerable and disadvantaged groups of people should be able to participate 'in an informed manner', it recommends.[6]

'Speaking as someone whose farm is to be flooded by a dam, the key recommendations of the report are that no dam should be built without the agreement of the directly affected people', said Sadi Baron, coordinator of Brazil's Movement of Dam Affected People.[7] If this recommendation is taken seriously, it could spell the end of large dams. For if people threatened by such a dam are allowed to participate they may persuade the authorities that there is a better way to proceed.

'The report vindicates much of what dam critics have long argued', said Patrick McCully of the California-based International Rivers Network. 'If the builders and funders of dams follow its recommendations, the era of destructive dams should come to an end. Alternatives do exist'.[8]

Large dams cost money and usually only proceed with funding from financial agencies such as the World Bank. While they have provided only 15 per cent of large dam funding, 'these institutions played a key strategic role globally in spreading the technology, lending legitimacy to emerging dam projects', says the report (see also Chapter 15). One of the worst aspects of large dam schemes is that they often undermine traditional and indigenous irrigation practices (see pp. 73–4). And often they have commanded resources that could have been used for decentralised small-scale dams.

Little dams: a success story

Small-scale irrigation is one of the success stories in developing countries, contrasting sharply with large-scale dams. Small-scale systems have often been developed by farmers in response to family and local market requirements. They include small dams, water tanks and shallow wells, valley bottom irrigation, minor stream diversion and rainwater catchment schemes.

There are millions of small-scale dams in developing countries, some of them part of micro-hydro schemes (a plant between 10 kW and 100 kW). Such dams have shown that they can tap rivers and lakes for irrigation and improve agricultural production in a more sustainable manner than large dams. They are also more likely to benefit the very poor. Micro-hydro schemes are again more likely to be developed in collaboration with the local community, which contributes civil costs, labour, some initial investment and is responsible for their maintenance and upkeep.

As well as irrigation, micro-hydro schemes are more likely to deliver electricity to people who live close by. 'Estimates of poverty reduction from micro-hydro … systematically understate poverty impact, as they exclude a range of very difficult to measure but important effects such as time savings from no longer having to carry kerosene or other fuel, improved education from the availability of electric light and improved health'.[9]

Small-scale dam schemes work in different ways. At the simplest level, earth embankments are placed across rivers to make a pond. Pumps and water wheels can be used. In the Indian state of Uttar Pradesh, for example, one local farmer has built a water-wheel pump from locally available materials. This requires no diesel or electricity; its only source of energy is the flow of water. The system is capable of irrigating 5,000 hectares of land. The water wheel is installed on a fast-flowing river and moved by the force of the water. With the use of the gears it runs at a speed which drives a centrifugal pump, in the same way that a pump might be driven by electricity or diesel. A small dam is created and also a reservoir. The pump draws water from the reservoir and a pipe connected to the pump takes the water to the fields – it can take it up to 10 km from the reservoir.[10]

An FAO report highlights how food security could be boosted by an increased use of locally produced low-cost treadle pumps. Easy to handle, such pumps can contribute to higher food production and create employment and income. Case studies from Kenya, Niger, Zambia and Zimbabwe show that by using treadle pumps farmers could increase irrigated land, improve crop quality, grow new crops and increase the number of cropping cycles. 'The economic benefits of small pumps have been significant for farmers. In Zambia, incomes have risen more than sixfold from US$125 achieved with bucket irrigation on 0.25 hectares of land to US$850–1,700 using treadle pumps. In some cases cropping intensity could be extended to three crops per year. In Zimbabwe, treadle pumps are mostly used for irrigation of small vegetable gardens. As a result, family nutrition has improved in most areas'.[11]

HARVESTING WATER

Techniques for harvesting water were developed by the Nabateans over 3,000 years ago in what is today Israel, Palestine and Jordan. 'It is probably not a coincidence that very similar techniques have been developed and have survived in the Red Sea Hills of North-west Sudan and in the central Darfur region'.[12] Ancient rubble dams found in Saurashtra, northwest India, could have been used for collecting water 5,000 years ago.

Water harvesting techniques are today being successfully employed by millions of small-scale farmers and have considerable further potential. Farmer-controlled and environmentally sound, they offer many people the most convenient and affordable route to using water for irrigation and higher food output.

The starting point is harvesting and storing the rainwater that falls on the roofs of houses, sheds and other buildings. Rainwater is easy to collect and store; farmers can build their own collection and storage system at low cost and under family control. A sloping roof, a pipe or gutter to carry the rainwater to a container is helpful, but if a roof is flat a panel can be erected at an angle to direct the rain downwards. Once in the container, water can be applied to crops and given to livestock as required.

There is an increasing recognition that water stores can be as important as grain stores. 'We started to build different types of tanks, underground tanks for irrigation and watering of animals, and various kinds of above-ground stores for drinking water', says John Mbugua, a water consultant of a rainwater harvesting project in the

Laikipia district of Kenya; 'several years later we see a changed area, because the water improves the conditions of living in so many ways'.[13] In the Laikipia project it was women's groups who adopted the technology. The women no longer have to spend long hours fetching water and have more time for growing vegetables and for poultry farming.

On sloping land, rainwater that had been wasted previously can also be directed to family or community small-scale reservoirs. Again it can be harvested by run-off techniques – channelling rain falling onto an uncultivated area of sloping land towards a smaller area of crop land. This puts the area under crops to better use and can produce considerable output. In an extreme case, in a dry season in Botswana for example, maize grown on catchment areas was 800 kg per hectare, whereas in non-catchment areas it was only 7 kg.[14] In Burkina Faso, and other countries, rainfall on sloping fields is being directed to crop areas by means of funnelling stone walls.

In India, the crops on around 70 per cent of cultivated fields depend on rain for their growth. In Africa the figure is over 90 per cent. River/lake irrigation, even from small-scale dams, is out of reach. Harvesting water means that these countries' agriculture does not have to be entirely rainfed.

Harvesting water from the fog and from clouds is a promising technology and again not a new idea. 'African nomads and Adean people have long taken advantage of trees' natural water catching properties by collecting morning dew or using the water trapped by forest'.[15] Water from fog is collected in countries such as Dominican Republic, South Africa, Nepal, Chile and Peru.

In a dry mountainous area of northern Chile, for example, fine nylon nets with very small holes have been mounted perpendicular to the windflow. When the clouds reach the panels, small drops of water are captured by the nets and then channelled through a plastic conduit to a closed container. From there, the water is channelled to more containers, cleaned with filters and distributed to households. This innovative type of water supply fulfils the needs of impoverished communities for the irrigation of agricultural plots and for drinking water.[16]

PUTTING FLOODS TO USE

In rural African economies, indigenous irrigation systems involve the integration of valley and upland environments, the physical management of soil and the practice of intercropping. The most basic method is cropping on rising and falling floods in wetland environments. Farming on a rising flood involves planting before the flood arrives and harvesting either after the flood has fallen, or from boats. Farming on a falling flood involves the use of residual soil moisture left by retreating floods. Banks are constructed to trap receding water in backswamp areas and pools, and suitable crops are planted.

In the floodplains, agriculture, fishing and grazing are closely integrated. Though flood cultivation is a high-risk activity, it offers the opportunity for high returns. Farmers deal with risk through crop and variety selection skills, planting crops with different requirements together in the same field, for example. They also have a detailed appreciation of the variation in land types in the floodplain and knowledge of past flooding patterns. Often farmers are also fishermen and/or herders or dryland cultivators.

One of the most extensive areas of flood-related cropping in West Africa is the Niger Inland Delta. Here, agriculture involves the flood cropping of sorghum and rice, also rainfed bullrush millet on un-flooded land. Where wells can reach the water table, rainfed crops may be followed by irrigated crops in small gardens. Sorghum is planted on the falling flood in January, often with other crops such as cassava or groundnuts. Rice is planted in the rains in July and August, grows with the rising floodwater and is harvested as the floods recede between December and February.

Many of Sub-Saharan Africa's rivers support wetlands of great ecological and human importance. In semi-arid areas seasonal high water levels cause extensive flooding which gradually falls with the river until, in the dry season, rivers can be reduced to pools of water separated by dry land. In the floodplain of the Senegal river, for example, 5,000 square kilometres are covered with water when it floods, which subsequently shrinks to 500 square kilometres in the dry season. Rainfall here is not only seasonal but also variable in space and time within a season. Against this unique climatic and ecological background, local communities have developed indigenous water management systems that are rooted in local culture.

'Modern' water management systems, by contrast, are often technology-based, relying heavily on foreign tools and know-how, demanding 'management' of nature and people: for instance, the need to control rivers by dams and barrages. Water for hydroelectric generation is often given higher importance than water intended for agriculture. This is illustrated by the case of the Lagdo Dam along the River Benue which flows from Cameroon into Nigeria. When the dam was closed to fill the reservoir in 1982, discharge of the Benue fell to a mere 43 per cent, despite it being a wet year. While the flood depth was reduced to a quarter of pre-dam levels, the flood lasted for only 3–15 days compared to a normal flood of 93–160 days. This caused havoc for the farmers downstream who were dependent on flooding patterns for their livelihood.

In the Senegal valley, the Manantali Dam upstream and associated irrigation development projects have been the cause for conflict between farmers and herders and serious ethnic violence between Senegal and Mauritania. Similarly in the floodplain of the Hadejia and Jama'are rivers in Nigeria, shrinkage of wetlands due to drought and the construction of the Tiga Dam in the 1970s to supply irriga- tion upstream have led to conflicts between seasonal pastoralists and local farmers.

> The undermining of indigenous knowledge systems has weakened the resilience of local communities in Sub-Saharan Africa; they do not have control over the new technological tools thrust on them, nor do they have control over their crops and their produce. As such, the flexibility necessary to cope with problems brought on by climatic changes such as drought is greatly compromised.[17]

DRAINAGE IS VITAL

Drainage is vital if irrigated land is not to be become degraded. Unless there is proper drainage, irrigation water can cause water- logging and salinity build-up in soils; this has become especially problematic in some prime irrigated land in Pakistan, northern India and Sub-Saharan Africa.

Water-induced land degradation is leading to long-term declines in the very crops the irrigated water was supposed to be spurring into ever-increasing production. Intensively irrigated land leads to long-term declines in the soil's nitrogen supply, and this affects the ability of the soil to produce the same yields as before.

In many countries of Sub-Saharan Africa, soil salinity linked to irrigation and drainage is a serious problem In the Sokoto Basin in Nigeria the development of a dam and irrigation scheme at Bakolori, without consideration of the basin as a whole, has proved disastrous to farmers downstream. Food output and fish catches fell due to reduced wet-season flooding, cultivation of rice declined, and land was turned over from rice to the less productive crops of millet and sorghum. The economically important dry-season vegetable production was reduced, and farmers turned to dry-season labour migration, a traditional response to periods of drought and hardship.

> Poor water management leading to a steady accumulation of salts in the soil has damaged 60 million hectares, roughly one fourth of the world's irrigated land. For every hectare brought under irrigation during the 1980s in Sub-Saharan Africa, another went out of production due to salination and waterlogging. Now suffering reduced yields, this land requires costly reclamation; some of it will eventually have to be abandoned.[18]

The Sahelian countries of Burkina Faso, Mali, Mauritania, Niger and Senegal have suffered from the irrigation of rice-growing land without proper drainage. Since the 1980s, and the advent of World Bank/IMF structural adjustment programmes, the five countries have more than doubled their output of rice from irrigated areas along river banks. Much of the increase is not only unsustainable, however, but the way it has been achieved could damage the region's ability to produce rice in future.

Under the terms of their adjustment packages, the five countries were urged to sell off common land that was suitable for growing rice to private buyers. The effect of this was to encourage get-rich-quick merchants to come in and develop rice fields. But often they installed the cheapest form of irrigation, without drainage.

The effect has been catastrophic. Flooded rice grows in the Sahel, as in Asian and other countries, by standing in water, but the water has to be drained away regularly, ideally twice a week, and a new supply pumped in, otherwise the standing water can cause severe problems. To cut costs, many of the newcomers did not dig drainage canals but left the rice in the same water for 4 to 5 months – the normal growing period.

Bureaucrats and small traders are among those who have moved in to cultivate rice. Some of the cheap schemes are so poorly constructed they last for only one season. As salt builds up on the soil, a salt crust is created, making the soil useless for agriculture. After a year in one field, the 'quick profit' operators are then moving off to other fields. 'The cost of regenerating the fields affected could be so high as to make it uneconomic'.[19]

In July 1998 the FAO launched a major international initiative to improve irrigation and drainage in developing countries. Producing more food can be done 'through the intensification of rain-fed and irrigated agriculture', believes Arumugam Kandiah of the FAO. 'Irrigation more than doubles land productivity. Unfortunately, many irrigation systems are working poorly, due to bureaucratic interference, faulty management, lack of involvement of users and poor construction. In some cases up to 60 per cent of the water diverted for irrigation never reaches the crop'.[20]

Making Water Go Further

There is a long history of conflict between people over water when the resource is scarce. A way to lessen the conflict is to think in terms of using water twice, believes Dr Elias Salameh, Professor of Hydrology at the University of Jordan in Amman. 'We have to distinguish between water use and water consumption', says Professor Salameh. 'When we use water we don't need to consume it, we can recycle it'. Instead of using good quality water for irrigation, he argues, 'why not use it for household purposes first and then for agriculture?'[21] This must happen in the future, he believes: 'Within the next 15 to 20 years, most irrigation water should be used water'.

Recycling water can help to defuse the conflict between agriculture and households or industry. Treated, reused water from urban areas is already available for some of Jordan's farmers, for example. If, as expected, water becomes increasingly scarce, then the use of second-time-round water could be both inevitable and sensible. 'The challenge is to develop and introduce the necessary technologies for water and water waste systems; the traditional policy of developing new resources to satisfy needs is, in the case of Jordan, almost exhausted'.

In rural and peri-urban areas of some developing countries, sewage and waste water is now being used for irrigation. Local sewage is the only water source that millions have to irrigate their crops. While there are obvious health risks, there are also considerable benefits – crops such as vegetables thrive when watered with nutrient-rich sewage.

Studies by the Sri Lanka-based International Water Management Institute (IWMI), carried out in Mexico and Pakistan, found 'equal positive and negative aspects, with no clear-cut choices for policy or health practices'. The research in Mexico examined the advantages and disadvantages of using urban waste water for crop production in Mexico's water-scarce Guanajuato river basin. Here, waste water irrigation is crucial for farmers. 'The economic value of waste water used for irrigation represents a significant monetary benefit to both society and these water users'.

In Pakistan, 'the primary benefits are financial gains for local farmers who cultivate high value crops, and increased crop productivity without the need to purchase additional fertiliser'.[22] But the study reveals an accumulation of heavy metals in the waste-water irrigated soils, indicating that land will become unprofitable unless it is properly managed.

Building facilities to treat the sewage is often not an economic option. The IWMI is trying to identify conditions under which the benefits of waste water irrigation can be realised, 'while minimising the risk and associated costs for public health and environmental quality'.

DIGGING DEEPER – A SOLUTION?

Digging deeper for water for irrigation may have a role to play in some localities. In Bangladesh, for example, investment in ground-water

> was a key stimulant to rapid agricultural growth in the 1980s and early 1990s. Nearly 1.5 million hectares of land was newly irrigated after 1980, in significant part from private installation of shallow tubewells spurred by deregulation of tubewell imports. Although localised problems of ground-water mining have occurred, in most areas in Bangladesh further expansion of groundwater use within the bounds of natural recharge is possible. If dry season water scarcity worsens, investments to divert wet season river flows for artificial recharge of aquifers may become feasible, and could also reduce wet season flooding.[23]

But the practice can lead to severe environmental problems. 'For our water-intensive crops such as rice and sugar cane, we are going deeper and deeper underground', says Ashok Gulati, a director at the National Council for Applied Economic Research in India. 'In the modern part of India's Punjab, so much water is being pumped from wells, the water table is going down by one and a half feet per year'.[24]

PRODUCTIVITY AND PRICING

In most developing countries, irrigation water is free to the user. This can lead to farmers applying too much. Improved productivity of water use and better management of the resource, including rainfall, could make a contribution to boosting crop yields and output. 'In many agricultural areas it seems that the productivity of water can be doubled', believes the IWMI. Water savings and productivity gains can be achieved in several ways:

- more reliable water supply to irrigated areas
- precision irrigation-delivery technologies
- water recycling
- management systems that give feedback on the effectiveness of irrigation systems.

Researchers in Asia have found that if farmers decrease their water use on rice paddies, there would be little or no impact on yields. The argument for putting a price on water is that it would help to encourage efficient use, saving irrigation water and decreasing irrigated land's negative effects on the environment.

Official agencies such as the World Bank press the case for full-cost pricing of water. However, for the vast majority of small-scale farmers in developing countries, who do not have irrigation from rivers or lakes, the pricing of water is irrelevant. 'If they buy water they have even less to spend on basic food', says an International Fund for Agricultural Development (IFAD) report.[25]

Water scarcity could be one of the main obstacles to food security unless the resource is used wisely. Technologies and policies that enable water to reach the poor and be used efficiently, more than once if possible, urgently need to be implemented.

PROMOTING FARMER INVOLVEMENT IN IRRIGATION

The benefits of including farmers in irrigation planning are widely accepted. The Andean Community Irrigation Project is an example of 'good practice' useful for governments and development organisations interested in planning and implementing irrigation projects *with* farmers instead of *for* them.

The goal of the collaborating organisations – spearheaded by the Netherlands Development and Cooperation Service and the Ecuadorian Agricultural Service Central – was to create an irrigation system that meets the precise social and agricultural needs of this farming community and one that the farmers can manage themselves. They realised this would not be possible without the farmers' participation in all stages of the project process.

The Andean project's participatory approach to community irrigation design teaches some common lessons that can benefit communities across the developing world. For example:

• The use of visual and hands-on models to make the process more 'farmer friendly'. One of the challenges of involving farmers in planning was bridging the communication gap between irrigation engineers and rural people. In the Andean project, the farmers, who had a difficult time understanding topographical maps and technical jargon, found it easy to relate to the plastic models. The project leaders brought the models to them, in their villages, enabling men and women to ask questions, bring up concerns, and make suggestions in the comfortable context of community discussions.

- Requiring men and women to earn their rights to irrigation water by participating in the design, construction and management of the system.

Andean farmers have taken this democratic approach to building up water rights and ensuring community participation for centuries: you earn your rights with your hands and head, rather than just by paying dues.

Because many of the men have left in search of work outside the community, the majority of the farmers are women. Involving them in the planning was one of the major challenges of the project. Standard methods of encouraging community participation, like the distribution of leaflets and brochures, failed to capture this largely illiterate audience. Village meetings conducted in the native language of Quechua have proved much more effective. The project has also trained women to be irrigation leaders and promoters and provided them with technical skills. This acknowledges their role as irrigators and allows them to earn water rights on their own behalf and that of their families.

To share the lessons they learned with others in the Andean Region, the collaborating organisations documented their experiences on video tape and developed an irrigation project guide; this can be downloaded from the International Water Management Institute's website: http://www.iwmi.org

Source: IWMI.

CHAPTER 8

WHEN LAND IS LIFE

Buy land; they're not making it any more.

Mark Twain

For us the land is our life; we would defend it to the last
drop of our blood.

Filipino peasant

LAND TENURE: AN ISSUE THAT WON'T GO AWAY

Millions of rural people are either landless or work small plots on
which they have no security of tenure; others work as hired hands
on large farms for a meagre return. Too poor to buy land, they rank
among the poorest of the poor. Lacking security of tenure, farmers
may not be interested in working the land in a sustainable way; they
want to get as much as they can from the soil in the short run.

The effects of landlessness and land insecurity on people and the
environment can be devastating. Poverty and hunger is the first
consequence. In turn this can have a knock-on effect on the environment. The landless who live near tropical forests are more likely to
move in after the loggers and clear a small plot to grow crops; the
forest suffers and the land may only support crops for a short time.
Chemicals may be used indiscriminately, essential maintenance neglected and the ability of the land to produce for future generations
eroded.

When people have land, which they either own or farm under secure tenure, they are likely to grow more food. Security of land is therefore a determinant of food production. Sustainable agriculture can best be achieved when people have equitable rights to land in addition to other agriculture resources. Land security for the poor can mean food security.

On large landholdings in many developing countries, especially in Latin America, productivity is generally low. Estimates suggest that the productivity of smaller farms is 'at least twice that of the largest ones'.[1] Dividing large farms into smaller units not only gives land to the landless, it means that more food per hectare is usually produced. Land reform can increase employment as well as productivity and incomes, as small farms employ more people per hectare than large units.

Redistributive land reforms have helped to reduce poverty and advance food security in a number of developing countries. In Brazil 70 per cent of rural households own no land, while some estates are gigantic in size. But land reform is beginning to work. When land in the Piaui district of northeast Brazil was redistributed to small farmers, for example, it spurred a new interest among them. On rainfed farms, yields increased by between 10 and 40 per cent; on irrigated fields, they rose by between 30 and 70 per cent. Ownership of the land had given the farmers an incentive to invest in it and to farm it sustainably. In El Salvador a 10 per cent rise in land ownership has boosted income per person by 4 per cent.[2] In India, the states where poverty has fallen the fastest are those that have implemented land reform.

In Thailand, a close connection has been noted between a secure title to land and farmer confidence. Resistance to expropriation of land is often strongest in areas where organic agriculture is practised as part of the culture. Also, Thai people who were encroaching on forest land have been given security of tenure over that land; they are now planting trees to replace the old ones that have been axed. Most strikingly in China, the shift from large farms to smallholdings has witnessed an unprecedented rise in farm output, enabling millions to escape from poverty.

In Colombia the government has come under intense pressure from agricultural, mining and logging interests to open up more of its forests for exploitation. Instead of giving in to the pressure, the government embarked on a land reform programme, granting titles to the Indians of the Amazon; the reform covered some 18 million hectares of land. The Indians farm their forests intensively but sustainably and the granting of land title means that their forest habitats will be preserved for them to continue their practices.

Land reform in Zimbabwe has become controversial, with the issue being used for political purposes. But while progress has been slow, the gains of reform are being seen. The productivity of re-settled families in Zimbabwe is more than five times higher than communal households in similar areas.

If such examples could be replicated throughout the developing world then a substantial increase in food output is possible from existing lands – and there is little 'new' land in the world to bring into production. When those who farm the land own it they work it well, but when outsiders own land they may not work it in a sustainable way, and the situation is perceived by those who farm it as unjust. 'Historically, genuine land reforms have led to greater agricultural production because they have redressed the inefficiencies of inequality', point out Frances Moore Lappé and Joseph Collins.[3] The example from the Philippines (see pp. 89–90) shows the value of participation, coordination and partnerships in land reform.

The advantages of redistributive land reform are being recognised by a growing number of countries. In eastern and southern Africa for example, 'only those states at war with themselves have not embarked upon directive tenure reform'.[4]

In conflict-afflicted countries, land may be contaminated with landmines that can explode and maim or kill at the touch of a foot. People are reluctant to grow food on such land. It can take only two or three mines to make a whole area suspect. Good farming land lies idle as a result. In 2001 this was a particular problem in some of the very poorest countries, including Afghanistan, Angola, Cambodia and Somalia. Even without landmines, agriculture in conflict-stricken countries is often severely disrupted. War means land out of use.

Slow Progress

In conflict-free countries, progress in providing the landless with land and security of tenure is often slow. Large landowners have used their muscle to block land and agrarian reform programmes. In Latin America, which has the world's most unequal land system, severe land inequality persists even after land reforms. However in both India and Pakistan, change has taken place following small farmers' insistence on their rights. In rural India, although the power of landlords is strong, village women have empowered themselves in some areas by forming their own organisation, enabling them to get better access to land.

Neither will land reform alone necessarily reduce inequality. Reform needs to be community-driven, tailored to local conditions with the poor being put at the centre of the process. Women may be unable to acquire land in their own right through the market. It is therefore important to give women more control over land – 'this can give them more power in the community and reduce their vulnerability in the household'.[5]

At the end of the 1990s it seemed that land reform projects were among donor favourites. The World Bank has taken the lead in promoting, and in some cases financing, land tenure reforms in countries such as South Africa, Guatemala, Honduras, Mexico, Colombia, Brazil, the Philippines, Thailand, Indonesia and India. In December 1999, for example, the World Bank announced approval of a US$202.1 million loan for land reform in Brazil to operate across all northeastern states. The Bank claims that the reforms will help increase the incomes of about 50,000 rural poor and peri-urban families by boosting agricultural output.

As landless people have little or no money to buy land, a question for governments is whether to acquire land for redistribution, or whether to encourage its sale on the open market, providing beneficiaries with grants or loans to buy it. Zimbabwe, Namibia and South Africa have taken the market approach, although the slow progress of reform in Zimbabwe has led to land invasions.

There are growing doubts as to whether market-assisted land reform is enough. Land is 'more than a commodity', stresses the

international peasant movement, Via Campesina, and land reform
'does not guarantee comprehensive agrarian reform'.[6] Greater emphasis is now being laid on this much wider issue. Alongside land
tenure and redistribution, agrarian reform embraces issues such as
access to credit, savings and markets in rural areas. Potentially this is
a much more powerful weapon against food insecurity. It enables
people to make the best use of land they have received. 'Agrarian
reform has to provide access to land, enable people to make use of
that land, security of tenure and the prospect of sustainability', con-
cluded participants at a 'Soil is Life' conference.[7]

'Agrarian reform is very much a live issue. It's on the political
agenda in many countries in Asia, Latin America and Southern Africa
as a strategy for achieving greater equity and social justice as well as
growth and development for large numbers of poor people', said a
statement of participants at a conference in the Philippines on agrarian
reform and rural development in January 2001.[8]

A wide consensus emerged at the conference on the 'positive
contribution' that more equal access to land and other resources can
make in the fight against poverty. 'Meaningful reform must involve a
significant transformation of property rights and ensure access to the
means to make agriculture more productive and sustainable ...
agrarian reform must involve state regulation to overcome the failure
of markets to deliver equitable, just and productive outcomes in
agriculture and rural development'.

THE WORLD BANK UNDER FIRE

While aid donors such as the World Bank are keen to push land
reform, they seem less willing to support far-reaching agrarian reform.
A report in June 2001 by the NGO Food First assesses the Bank's
approach to land reform. It applauds the recognition by Bank
economists that 'extremely inequitable access to productive resources
like land prevents economic growth', but expresses serious concerns
about the reliance on land privatisation and free market forces. These
approaches are 'fast bringing civil society into conflict with the Bank',
it says. The report alleges that the Bank's approach, including the

privatisation of communal lands, 'can cause the breakdown of community-based resource management systems, leading to accelerated land degradation'. Also that 'land titling, registries, and facilitation of land markets can induce mass sell-offs of land, causing increased landlessness, land concentration, and rural–urban migration [and that] offering credit to landless farmers to buy land at market rates may lead to only the most marginal and most remote plots being sold and leave new landowners with heavy debts'.[9] The report recommends instead 'reform from below', as exemplified by the Brazilian Landless Movement, which has seized 15 million acres of land in recent years.

A study commissioned by South African civil society organisations and German Agro Action found that the 'concept of market-oriented agrarian and land reform has proved inadequate'. The World Bank's concept, it says, 'is only applicable to a limited degree, in circumstances in which labour-intensive agriculture is still regarded as backward'.[10] A petition to the World Bank on market-based land reform, prepared by Via Campesina and the human rights group Foodfirst Information and Action Network (FIAN), rejects 'the ideology that considers land only as a commodity'. The two organisations work with the National Forum on Agrarian Reform in Brazil and grassroots groups in the Philippines and South Africa.

In the declaration of an 'International Meeting of Landless Peasants', held in Honduras in July 2000, delegates from 24 countries stated: 'We observe with concern that the dominant agrarian policies, implemented within the framework of neo-liberalism, increasingly attempt to subject agrarian reform to the mechanics of the land market'.

The petition expresses 'deep concern' about the land reform policies being promoted by the World Bank since the mid-1990s. It says that the 'market-assisted land reform' provides beneficiaries with a combination of grants and loans which they use to negotiate the purchase of land from willing sellers and is supposed to be a more promising approach than using land reform agencies with powers of expropriation. The petition points out that this 'does not guarantee the realisation of an integrated and comprehensive agrarian reform since market-led land redistribution in oligopolistic environments is impossible. By implementing this model the Bank is failing to realise its own Operational Directive on Poverty Reduction. This has been illustrated by the results of such programmes so far which have not fundamentally altered the patterns of land ownership'.

Specific problems with the programmes include their failure to reach the poorest families, increases in land prices caused by the state credit supply, and the failure of the schemes to produce sufficient willing land sellers. Participation has also been inadequate: 'as the Brazilian experience illustrates, the Bank bypassed landless and small farmers' organisations at the national level' when drawing up its project. The petition concludes by asking the Bank for a suspension of support to further market-assisted land reform programmes and a re-examination of the market-assisted land reform model through a participatory monitoring process.[11]

Individualised forms of tenure may not be the best way to increase agricultural productivity and can even be counter-productive. African land tenure, for example, is characterised by the coexistence of customary and statutory rights. Access to land by rural people is not only essential for food production, it also maintains the fabric of social relations. As detailed in the last chapter, Sahelian countries were urged to sell off common land that was suitable for growing rice to private buyers. The effect of this was shoddy irrigation without drainage, which has seriously damaged the land.

Political will and government action are vital for redistributive land reform. 'Land reform cannot happen unless we have the political prerequisites for it', says Lino de David. 'Deep-rooted political change is needed if agrarian reform is to be achieved'. He believes that, without agrarian reform, the Amazon rainforest cannot be preserved, as people with no land will continue moving into forest areas.[12]

By the early 2000s another land issue was threatening livelihoods – landlessness was on the rise because of the impact of trade liberalisation and the flow of cheap food imports into developing countries. Unable to compete with these imports, small farmers are being forced out of business and land is being concentrated into larger holdings. Land reform in reverse is therefore occurring.[13]

LAND LOSS

Each year, globally, land abandoned due to *salinity* is about equal to
land developed for irrigation. It is difficult, expensive and slow to
improve saline or waterlogged land; techniques include moving soil
and installing drainage pipes.

The other source of loss is *erosion*, especially on slopes in arid and
semi-arid areas, and above all in Africa where, in 1992, 4 per cent of
the area under vegetation was seriously degraded and 18 per cent lightly
degraded — about half of this is due to overgrazing. Techniques for
reclaiming degraded land include earth or stone contour bunds, water
harvesting, digging and refilling pits and planting appropriate vegetation erosion barriers or species. (See also chapters 5 and 13.)

Source: *Rural Poverty Report*, 2001. Rome: IFAD, p. 145.

Cambodia is among the countries affected. More and more land
has been bought and sold, leaving farmers with not enough or no
land to support their livelihoods. 'Ten years after what was considered a reasonably fair distribution of land at the onset of the adoption of liberal market economy in 1989, it is estimated that between
10 and 15 per cent of farmers are landless. We witness land being
concentrated in the hands of fewer farmers'.[14]

The benefits of agrarian reform are therefore in danger of being
offset by wider international factors. In Chile the boom in exports
of fruit from the country's central valley, which started in the early
1970s, at least partially reversed the impacts on land structure of a
1968 land reform. Smallholders who had benefited from the land
reform could not make the large initial investments in fruit trees and
were rarely able to obtain credit. They lost out to larger landowners
who could make the necessary investment.

Despite the compelling arguments for agrarian reform that would
help people who are food insecure, implementation remains slow in
many countries — 'delayed or manipulated by the power of vested
interests'.[15] In other cases the lack of 'beneficiary participation' has
limited the impact and sustainability of reforms, says an IFAD report.

Agrarian reform has the potential to make a significant contribution to food security, but participation of the landless and the land insecure is vital, as is the attention to international factors which can put agrarian reform into reverse.

LAND REFORM IN THE PHILIPPINES

Land reform in the Philippines was moving slowly until a new partnership transformed prospects. In 1988 the Philippine government promised in its Comprehensive Agrarian Law Reform (CALR) to distribute more than 10 million hectares of both public and private lands to almost the same number of landless farmers over a ten-year period. The law also provided for a participation of non-governmental organisations, people's organisations and other sectors in the implementation of CALR.

However, after more than a year of implementation, leaders from key NGO networks, academe, peasant movements, the donor community and a segment from the Department of Agrarian Reform observed that things were not moving as envisaged. Lands were not being transferred, various government agencies did not coordinate. Funds for support services were being misused. Corruption in high places involved land deals. NGOs were not involved in the process at that stage.

Thus, in 1989, the Philippine Partnership for the Development of Human Resources in Rural Areas (PhilDHRRA), a 66-member NGO network, catalysed the establishment of Tripartite Partnership for Agrarian Reform and Rural Development or TriPARRD. Designed to help speed up the process and ensure the implementation of agrarian reform, the programme was launched in 28 prototype agrarian reform communities in three strategically located provinces (Camarines Sur, Antique, and Bukidnon) involving initially 13 province-based NGOs, seven government agencies, a national peasant organisation called PAKISAMA, four leading academic institutions and two NGO donor agencies.

By 1995 the programme had expanded into two other provinces (Iloilo and Davao del Norte), and helped to influence the overall strategy of the government Agrarian Reform Programme, mainstreaming the tripartite approach in agrarian reform implementation in all 70 provinces of the Philippines. This shows the potential that exists to uplift the lives of several hundreds of thousands of small-scale farmer households.

The TriPARRD programme has drawn persons from separate organisations into clusters that aggregated, disaggregated, and re-aggregated, with all contributing to and undergoing the learning process in making agrarian reform get ahead. The programme hoped that the experiences in the pilot provinces and sites would transcend these localities to energise a whole network of fluid, albeit committed, groups that would push agrarian reform to become an unstoppable movement. The incorporation of the TriPARRD principles in the government's on-going programme of building productive agrarian reform communities promises the realisation of this hope.

For agrarian reform to be carried out democratically it is necessary that:

- Landless women and men farmers at farm household level are transformed into owner-cultivators
- Landless farmers are able to access and manage human, natural and material resources both locally and externally
- Landless farmers are able to improve their productivity systems in a sustainable fashion.

The programme concentrated on distributing big privately owned lands, both those voluntarily offered for sale and those subject to compulsory purchase, in 28 prototype communities. The programme was not successful in transferring all the lands but was able to transfer 68 per cent after five years in the initial three provinces.

Many farmers who have secured their (land) titles have started to diversify their crops, using ecologically friendly agricultural practices. Farmers in the 60 prototype areas have been organised, mostly into associations then transformed later into cooperatives. They have developed the capacity to deal with the bureaucracy in a more creative manner ... to solve agrarian problems.

Source: Marlene Ramirez, 'Cooperation boosts land reform', *International Agricultural Development*, March/April 1996.

CHAPTER 9

WOMEN FOOD PRODUCERS:
RELEASING THEIR POTENTIAL

There will no food security without rural women.
Jacques Diouf, Director-general, FAO

Without women we all go hungry.
Ancient African proverb

In Western countries a typical farmer could be a hefty man in a grimy pair of overalls sitting on a tractor. In developing countries, the typical farmer is more likely to be a woman, planting seeds or weeding a field, with a baby on her back.

Many of the problems facing small-scale farmers and the rural poor are common to both women and men. But a traditional gender divide in which men grow crops for export and women grow most of the food crops often leads to specific problems for women. But agricultural policies in developing countries have generally been framed for male, not female, farmers, and can create additional burdens for females.

Releasing the potential of women farmers is vital if food security is to be achieved. Frequently overlooked by policymakers, women produce 60 to 80 per cent of the staple food crops in most developing countries. In Sub-Saharan Africa and the Caribbean, the figure is nearer 80 per cent of staple food production. In Asia, women perform up to 90 per cent of the work in the rice fields. They work longer hours than men when producing food – 'on average [women] work

13 hours more than men each week in Asia and Africa. In Uganda they work more than twice as long'.[1]

Rural women are the main producers of the world's chief staple foods: rice, wheat and maize. Their contribution to secondary crop production, such as legumes and vegetables, is even greater. With detailed knowledge of many crops – such as how the different parts of a plant can be used for food, medicine and animal feed – women are central to the selection, breeding, cultivation, preparation and harvesting of food. They have a key role to play in protecting and saving the seeds (and breeding stock) that provide the 'genetic resources' for producing food. For example, in the Andean region of South America, women collect and store seeds in 'seed banks' on which their food production relies. Their specialised knowledge about genetic resources for food and agriculture makes them vital custodians of biodiversity.

Women sow, weed, apply fertiliser and pesticides, harvest and thresh the crops, and after harvesting provide most of the labour for post-harvest activities. Millions have the responsibility of storing, handling, stocking, processing and marketing the crops. In the live-stock sector, women feed and milk the larger animals, while raising poultry and small animals such as sheep, goats, rabbits and guinea pigs. Women often possess unique knowledge about the fisheries sector; in many developing countries they do most of the inland fishing and handle the work associated with fish farming.

Gender Bias – Despite Women's Increasing Role

Furthermore, the role of women in food-crop agriculture in developing countries is increasing as fewer men are now farmers. Economic circumstances are often forcing men to leave rural areas and seek work and an income in towns and cities. Rural male populations are also declining because of sickness and war. The spread of HIV/AIDS has led to a rise in the numbers of female-headed households in the developing world, placing a considerable burden on women's capacity to produce, provide and prepare food.

While their role is essential to improving nutrition and enhancing living conditions, women farmers usually number among the very poorest. Often they are more vulnerable than men to malnutrition 'because of their different physiological requirements', says a UN Food and Agriculture Organisation (FAO) report. 'In most cases, a woman requires a higher intake of vitamins and minerals in proportion to total dietary energy intake than a man'.[2]

Women farmers not only generate income through farming, processing and marketing of their goods, they also bear chief responsibility for the health and wellbeing of their family. In addition to working in the fields, they normally have the task of collecting wood and water and preparing food for their families. 'An important finding of research in recent years is that women invest more than men in household food security. This is despite the fact that the income earned by women ... tends [to be] quite low', finds a study of Ethiopia. In particular it seems that women are more likely to use income to improve their family's nutrition.[3]

Despite their central contribution to food security, women farmers tend to be underestimated and overlooked in development strategies. They remain the 'invisible' partners. Because of the way that national income statistics are calculated, the food they produce for the family does not count – it is not given a monetary value. By contrast the food that male farmers produce for the market does count. Policy-makers are too often aware only of the statistics and do not fully appreciate the role of women.

With their contribution under-counted and undervalued, women farmers often receive fewer services than their male counterparts. They normally have less access than males to key resources such as land, water, credit and extension services – receiving, for example, only 5 per cent of all agricultural extension services worldwide.

Studies by the FAO show that women have been the last to benefit from economic growth and development and in some cases have been negatively affected:

> Gender bias and gender blindness persist: farmers are still generally perceived as male by policy-makers, development planners and agricultural service deliverers. For this reason, women find it more difficult than men to gain

access to valuable resources such as land, credit and agricultural inputs, technology, extension, training and services that would enhance their production capacity.[4]

Gender bias varies. It is common in customary laws in Latin America and the Caribbean, whereas in the highlands of Asia and the Pacific 'women suffer less discrimination than do those in the rest of the region'.[5] But the specific needs of women farmers are widely ignored in development planning and projects. Development projects can work against women, helping men at their expense. While, for example, an increase in the output of the food crop cassava is welcome, it means more work for women, who have the lengthy task of processing the cassava. 'Evaluations have shown that if gender specificities are not taken into account, projects may increase women's workload, thus affecting their caregiving responsibilities and health. Projects may also negatively affect women's control over resources and technologies'.[6]

Many development projects have paid little attention to women farmers. Despite the sentiments of its Director-general, less than 1 per cent of FAO projects 'include strategies for reaching women; in the UN system as a whole less than 4 per cent of projects benefit women'.[7]

WHAT NEEDS TO CHANGE?

Empowerment

Cultural norms mean that women in many countries are excluded from participating in decisions affecting both their households and communities. In Sub-Saharan Africa it is usually men who decide what tools to buy, even though women are the main agricultural labourers. A greater understanding of the role of women farmers is needed, both among policymakers and male farmers. There needs to be a greater appreciation that releasing the potential of rural women could make a substantial contribution to food security.

The empowerment of women is vital for increasing food output, raising levels of nutrition, improving the distribution of food and agricultural products and the living conditions of rural populations. Cultural, traditional and sociological factors that limit women's access to resources are likely to be increasingly questioned as women's access to education rises. Increased educational opportunities should lead to change that improves both the status and incomes of women.

An FAO Plan of Action for Women in Development, which ran from 1996 to 2001, aimed to give women 'equal access to and control of land and other productive resources, increase their participation in decision- and policy-making, reduce their workloads and enhance their opportunities for paid employment and income'.[8] But only limited progress was achieved.

If women are to be empowered, they need more gender-sensitive policies from government, greater access to educational facilities, to resources such as water and credit and the right kind of technology. More research into their specific problems and needs is also vital. And it is important to focus on gender, rather than solely on women, stresses an IFAD report, 'in order to include men in project initiatives and promote the sustainability of these activities'.[9]

Education

A recent World Bank study found that if women received the same education as men, farm yields could rise by as much as 22 per cent. In Kenya, a national information campaign targeted at women increased yields of maize by 28 per cent, beans by 80 per cent and potatoes by 84 per cent. In countries where females have similar educational opportunities, Burkina Faso for example, they farm land more productively than males. 'Giving women one year of education can lead to an estimated 24 per cent increase in yields'.[10]

But illiteracy often excludes people from written knowledge, decision-making and employment. A girl may be deprived of schooling and literacy for no other reason than being female. Seventy per cent of poor women in India cannot read or write. The type of work that rural women do 'is limited by their low education levels and lack of decision-making authority within the household'.[11]

Access to resources and markets

Access to credit is seldom feasible let alone affordable for women farmers. With fewer assets, a woman farmer is less likely than a male to obtain credit to buy essential equipment and farm inputs. Access to inputs is important – it has been estimated that if female maize farmers could obtain the same level of inputs as males, their yield would rise by 9 per cent.[12] A study of Zambia found that if women were to have the same degree of capital investment in agricultural inputs as men 'output would increase by up to 15 per cent'.[13]

But a woman may not be able to offer land as collateral. In many societies a woman cannot inherit or legally own land. Land reforms schemes have generally not helped; very few traditional or reformed land allocation systems have significantly raised women's control over land.

The 1990s witnessed the spread of more credit facilities to women farmers (see Chapter 10) but little progress on access to land. Denying women the right to land is basically unjust, especially in view of the growth of female-headed, one-adult households. Such households comprise over a quarter of rural households in many developing countries and are increasing rapidly; in some areas in rural India, for example, they increased from 20 per cent in 1970 to 35 per cent in 1996.

A farmer who has children to care for may not be as mobile as a woman or man in a two-adult household. Travelling long distances to buy agricultural inputs, or to take produce to market, may be difficult. In this situation, decentralised, local systems are essential.

Technology and research

Growing the right kind of crops, plus appropriate, environmentally friendly, labour-saving devices could do much to assist women farmers. The introduction of legume crops, for example (see pp. 98–9), can make an important contribution. Devices to help with weeding would be helpful. Weeding has been described as 'the most time-consuming and probably also the most energy-demanding activity in the entire farm operation'.[14] Equipment such as the hand cultivator can help reduce the weeding burden.

Improved methods of pounding cereals could again do much to reduce the working hours of women farmers. When cereal milling machines were introduced into villages in Gambia, for example, women were saved the laborious job of pounding the staple food, millet, by hand. One woman told me that some of the time saved she now spends in the field, planting maize and beans and earning a cash income for the first time.[15]

Improved crop-drying methods, such as solar dryers for vegetables, could make a contribution – as could improved smoking techniques. Post-harvesting technology, including appropriate storage facilities, could again help women farmers. But more research is needed into the specific problems they face. Formal research has often paid little attention to women's knowledge, although scientists are at least starting to recognise their role in agriculture and the need to work with women in conducting agricultural research. Gender analysis techniques are now being used to make agricultural research more relevant to women farmers – efforts that include developing crops that grow rapidly, cook easily and are higher in protein and other basic nutrients.[16]

Extension

Extension staff give advice to farmers, sharing with them new ways of doing things, new thoughts and ideas. But extension staff are overwhelmingly male even in countries where women produce most of the food; in most developing countries women make up only a tiny proportion of the staff. As a result the advice that women receive is often male-oriented and inappropriate. 'In very few countries has an adequate organisational structure been found for advising rural women who work in the fields'.[17] As women farmers have working problems that are often specific to them, it is important to increase the numbers of female advisors. Where these exist at village level – in Cameroon for example – women farmers often feel the advice they receive is based on a better understanding of their problems. Increased opportunity to attend agricultural colleges and obtain the right qualifications is also vital if more trained female staff are to be available.

GENDER AND GENETIC ENGINEERING

Genetic engineering 'will rob Third World women of their creativity, innovation and decision-making power in agriculture. In place of women deciding what is grown in fields and served in kitchens, agriculture based on globalisation, genetic engineering and corporate monopolies on seeds will establish a food system and world view in which men controlling global corporations control what is grown in our fields and what we eat. Corporate men investing financial capital in theft and beepers will present themselves as creators and owners of life. We do not want a partnership in this violent usurpation of the creativity of creation and Third World women by global biotechnology corporations who call themselves the Life Sciences Industry even while they push millions of species and millions of small farmers to extinction'.

Source: Vandana Shiva, speech to Women in Agriculture conference, Washington, June/July 1998.

A vicious circle

Greater investment in rural women could do much to help food security. Schooling for girls can lead to a reduction in poverty, giving women the literacy skills and confidence to have their say about how things are run. A mother's education often leads to better health and nutrition for her children. More investment in improving the lot of rural women could create a virtuous circle of better education, improved health and higher incomes. And women need to be given the right to have more control over productive assets – of land, water and credit, for example. Removing gender inequalities is not only morally right, it is good for economic growth and development.

WOMEN FARMERS AND LEGUMES IN ZAMBIA

Women in Zambia's Northern Province have banded together and found a way to ensure their families get a healthier diet and that they increase their incomes. The key lies in growing legume crops like cowpeas and soybean.

Planting the legumes takes place on communal plots organised by women's clubs. The women usually spend one day a week nurturing their crops, then the rest of the week in their own fields tending the country's staple crop, maize. 'My family only gets meat once a month, usually chicken, so these cowpeas are a good idea for us. They're tasty in stew with meat or by themselves as a relish with maize', says Emma Mwansa, secretary of the Tubombe women's club, which now has 26 members.

Such clubs work alongside non-governmental organisations that distribute improved seed varieties and provide training. This is a key part of a country-wide integrated crop management/food legume project (funded by the UN Development Programme and the Zambian government with assistance from FAO). The project aims to introduce drought-resistant legumes that also return nutrients to the soil and can grow vigorously without heaps of expensive fertiliser.

Legume crops are also ideally suited to the small-scale farming carried out by the women. The only other protein for these women and their families comes from groundnuts or bambara nuts. Overlooking the women's quarter-hectare field of cowpeas, which is scrupulously clear of weeds and flourishing, Emma Mwansa says, 'We should have enough cowpea for the whole year for our families, plus some for seed for next season to give back to the seed loan'.

The seeds are distributed like this: having bought seed from the project, NGOs lend it to individual farmers or farmers' groups. Five-kg bags are enough to sow a quarter of an hectare. The farmers then have to repay 10 kg of seed. The NGOs then pass the paid-back seed loan on to the next group of farmers.

'We're trying to make them self-reliant', said Marleen Kramer, a coordinator of the NGO Development Organisation for People's Empowerment. 'Once the club gets one lot of seed, they won't get the same type again. They have to succeed with the seed they hold back for themselves or which they trade with other clubs'. Women's clubs are hoping for good returns. Typically, it is hoped that the crop surplus will be around 270 kg, which can be consumed locally or sold on the market where there is strong demand.

Farmers hope to make a good return. 'This soybean is much more profitable than other crops. The price is good and we don't have the expense of fertiliser', said Stephenia Chimfwembe, who heads the women's club in the village of Aluni. 'If we make a profit this year, we'll expand the fields and add groundnuts and beans. But we'll plant earlier to avoid the bird problem we had this time', she added.

Source: FAO website: www.fao.org.

CHAPTER 10

THE CREDIT LINE

Creditors have better memories than debtors

J. Howell

Millions of resource-poor small-scale farmers do not have access to credit or savings facilities. The use of credit, in the form of a loan from a bank or other finance institution, can help their farming activity. It can however also take farmers down wrong paths and trap them in debt.

The case for saving and credit facilities is nonetheless strong. Small-scale farmers may have few or no liquid resources of their own to buy even a small amount of inputs such as seed. Unless they are on a strict permaculture 'no outside input' system, this can be a serious drawback. Traditional ways of saving, such as putting money into livestock or jewellery, leave them in a weak position when they need cash.

The 1990s witnessed a rapid growth of microfinance institutions in developing countries, giving farmers access to savings facilities to enable them to deposit money when they had it, for example after selling their harvested crops, or being able to withdraw it in times of need, and qualify for a loan when the occasion arose. A savings account can also help farmers in obtaining insurance, giving a sense of security.

Credit facilities are generally not extended to resource-poor farmers, however, even for highly productive activities, because they have few or no assets to offer a bank as collateral. But those who have borrowed small amounts have often seen their incomes rise; they also generally have a sound record of repaying their loans.

Although microfinance institutions have spread to most developing countries, the numbers covered by savings and credit schemes remains small. In 1997 the World Bank estimated that there were over 7,000 microcredit programmes serving 16 million people in the developing world – less than 1 per cent of the population. The institutions include community-run rural banks, savings and credit cooperatives and grassroots organisations of indigenous origin. A 'microcredit summit' organised in 1997 by Results Education, a US-based NGO, launched a campaign to extend these facilities to 100 million people by 2005.

There are, however, a number of problems over the availability of microfinance. Many financial institutions still do not recognise that resource-poor farmers need to borrow money. These farmers may find banks intimidating places and have difficulty conforming with requirements, such as attending meetings; while many banks take the view that small, micro-lending is unprofitable because of the lack of collateral – no guarantee of repayment – and the limited amount loaned. The formal banking sector therefore sees dealing with the poor as barely economical.

Poor farmers may also be reluctant to take out a loan. With no reserves, even a small loan may be considered too big a risk. It is the better-off who are more likely to use microfinance and to benefit.

The bigger problem with microcredit is that success has yet to be proved. 'The evidence of the impact of microcredit is not clear-cut. Some research suggests that access to credit has the potential to reduce poverty significantly but there is also research suggesting that micro-credit has a minimal impact on poverty reduction'.[1]

MICROCREDIT: HOW IT WORKS

While microfinance facilities have been extended to small farmers and the rural poor, they have often failed to reach the people most in need. One of the first such facilities was the Grameen (village) Bank in Bangladesh. Set up in the mid-1970s by university economist Mohammed Yunus, this provides credit to the landless and those with small landholdings. It gives small loans – the average is around US$80 – to people who form 'solidarity groups'.

The Grameen Bank has five chief objectives: to extend banking facilities to poor men and women; to eliminate exploitation by moneylenders; to create opportunities for self-employment among the poor; to bring the disadvantaged into a structure they can understand and operate, and in which they can find sociopolitical and economic strength through mutual support; and finally to turn the vicious circle of 'low income, low savings, low investment, low income' into an expanding circle of 'more income, more credit, more investment, more income'. The bank lends to people with a cultivable land area of less than 0.4 acres.

The Grameen Bank has expanded into a sizable institution, lending around US$30 million a month to people in 22,000 out of Bangladesh's 68,000 villages. Over 90 per cent of borrowers are women. Although only a small proportion of bank loans are given directly for farming purposes, almost all the loans have an impact on the agricultural sector. Farm wages have risen by a quarter in Grameen Bank areas and the ability of traders to force down prices for postharvest agricultural produce has been substantially reduced. Traders who enjoyed a monopoly over stocking such produce are now forced to compete with many more small stockists from among the landless.

With good repayment rates, the Grameen Bank appears to have shown that the poor are bankable and the example has been widely replicated in other developing countries. But although the bank was originally considered a model of how credit can reach the poorest, one study found that only a fifth of Grameen's loans are to the landless 'in a country where the vast majority of the poor are landless'. This highlights the difficulty of getting credit into the hands of the people who most need it. Another project in Bangladesh, a state-run programme called TRDEP, classifies 70 per cent of its borrowers in the poor category, but 'methodically excludes the very poorest from its clientele'.[2]

Programmes that do succeed in bringing credit to the poor are likely to be informal. In parts of Africa and Asia, it is informal institutions that have been successful in mobilising savings and organising credit and insurance. The Country Women Association of Nigeria (COWAN), for example, is developing traditional African ways of banking – including the credit systems ESUSU and AAJO (rotational credit and savings and loan) – into what is known as African Traditional Responsive Banking (ATRB).

In ATRB, the policies for ownership, disbursement, guarantees, monitoring, security, recovery, interest, etc. were developed for the understanding, acceptance and participation of poor women. The system provides rural/urban poor women with access to loans without tears or fears. Formal banking system officials have now become partners in the ATRB. During its development process, adjustments were needed in both the formal and informal systems to pave the way for a new institution that would be recognised as a bank by the formal banking industry and African tradition.

In 1982 COWAN started operating in six villages in Ondo State, giving small loans to two groups of 50 women. By the mid-1990s COWAN was operating in 720 villages in 18 states in Nigeria, serving a total membership of about 78,600.

> COWAN has become a permanent engine of growth with equity through its five cardinal programmes which are: training, health care, credit, agriculture and technology. These programmes revolve round the development of human and natural resources and sustainable livelihoods in poor rural and urban areas. COWAN's integrated approach to hunger and sustainable population and environmental development, and most especially the development of ATRB, has made it an important element in today's system of economic development in our rural areas. ATRB has now brought to the economic development process rural women who do not ordinarily participate.[3]

In some credit schemes, for logical reasons it seems, people do not find it easy to qualify for loans. They may need to be physically fit. The Uganda Women's Effort to Save Orphans (UWESO), for example, assists grandparents and others who are caring for children orphaned by HIV/AIDS to set up 'economically viable income-generating projects'. With support from a European NGO, the Belgium Fund for Survival, UWESO runs a 'credit and savings scheme' that lends small amounts to carers, usually no more than £100. But Ugandan grandmother, Anna Nansubuga, is among those who do not qualify, even though she cares for 11 grandchildren, aged between 8 and 14.

Anna Nansubuga can only walk with difficulty, getting along with the help of a stick. She has land around her house but is too infirm to work it. Anna has no regular income and gets by with help from neighbours. Her physical infirmity makes it virtually impossible for her to embark on income-generating activity. She therefore does not qualify.[4]

Rates of interest charged by rural banks are sometimes too high for small-scale farmers. Higher-yielding varieties of cassava, for example, have become more widely available in Ghana in recent years. But farmers usually need credit to afford to buy cuttings of the new varieties. In Ghana's Ashanti region, the Otuasekan Rural Bank charges borrowers a 37 per cent rate of interest, which farmers say is too high for them to run a profitable farming operation.

Cassava is processed by women and the new varieties mean that they will handle two or three times more tubers than before. To help them, inexpensive, labour-saving cassava processing equipment is available on credit. But again the high borrowing rate is a deterrent.[5]

QUESTIONABLE CREDIT

By the 1990s, credit schemes had become part of many development projects. But questions were being raised over the purposes for which people were encouraged to borrow money under these projects. By definition, the taking out of credit means that farmers become indebted. If the loans work out, they can repay; if not, then farmers with few or no reserves can be in serious difficulty and a project that is supposed to help them may end up doing the opposite.

Credit seems to be a favourite for the World Bank because it encourages people to move away from subsistence farming and embrace the market economy. But this can mean that inputs such as pesticides and 'improved' seeds are purchased, which may not be the right strategy for the resource-poor. World Bank credit has also enabled farmers to move into producing export crops which are already in oversupply on world markets. This happened in Vietnam in the

1990s. In the early 1990s Vietnam's farmers were constrained from diversifying into export crops like coffee because of lack of money to buy inputs and the serious lack of credit in the rural areas. The World Bank stepped forward with a US$96m. loan for restructuring the agricultural sector 'with $50m. of the loan going to rural credit programmes'.[6]

For farmers this was the opportunity they sought. Coffee was seen as the 'green gold'. They took full advantage of the credit, bought and planted coffee trees, among others, expanding enormously the area under crop. Four years later the trees yielded their first harvest and Vietnam shot up the coffee producers' league to become the second largest – and the world coffee market collapsed. In 2000 the world price halved, to the distress of farmers who grow coffee in over 70 countries. For many of these farmers, coffee is their only income earner (see also Chapter 15).

The credit-encouraged move into coffee therefore had disastrous implications for coffee-growing farmers the world over; farmers in Vietnam discovered too late that their hopes of green gold had turned to dust.

Questionable credit has come also from, among others, the UN's International Fund for Agricultural Development (IFAD). Farmers in Mali, for example, were encouraged in the early 1980s to take out loans under an IFAD-funded project to grow maize. But when the rains failed in 1984, the maize harvest failed as the farmers had no irrigation. But they were expected to pay back the money they had borrowed. Again Malian farmers were given credit to help them grow peanuts for the export market. But the market mechanisms – the practical aspect of buying the peanuts from the farmers – were not put in place, leaving farmers with peanuts rather than cash. Again they were expected to repay their loans.

In Zambia, under the IFAD-funded North Western Province Area Development Project (NWPADP), loans of US$200 were accorded to farmers to help them buy hybrid maize seeds and fertilisers. Most farmers are engaged in subsistence agriculture, growing cassava, millet and sometimes beans; some also grow maize for the market as well as for their families. But many farmers considered a loan of $200 was too high a risk and it was the better-off farmers, those willing to take a risk, who received most of the credit. About 9,000 farmers in the province have received these loans (out of about 160,000 farming families). Repayment rates are low. A project evaluation shows that loan 'recoveries' were 46 per cent in 1992/3, 80 per cent in 1993/4, but only 10.7 per cent in 1994/5. Some farmers have been unable to repay because the inputs they have purchased under the loan scheme have been too 'high-tech' and not suitable.

The fertilised hybrid maize has not always given the extra yield over the traditional open-pollinated maize varieties of the province that would enable farmers to repay. Hybrid maize calls for a high degree of management, requiring skills which peasant farmers may not have. Most farmers cannot even get smaller loans, for example for fertiliser.[7]

The Challenge

There is an unsatisfied demand from small-scale farmers in developing countries for loans. Food production could be given a boost by an extension of microcredit to these farmers, provided loans are small-scale and appropriate for their needs. The type of microfinance institution that is needed will vary from country to country. The challenge is to develop informal institutions that are geared to helping people who are vulnerable to food insecurity.

Small loans are an important part of the answer. A New York-based organisation, Trickle Up, has given loans of around $50 with encouraging results over many years. When loans are smaller, the poorest have a chance of qualifying.

NGOs which have made low-cost credit schemes work should be invited to be part of every official development project that has a credit component. This would give projects a better chance of helping resource-poor farmers to increase their output and avoid potentially disastrous loans.

CHAPTER 11

RURAL DEVELOPMENT:
THE WIDER CONTEXT

Big ships are steered by very small rudders.
Book of James, Chapter 3, verse 4

Small-scale farmers and other rural dwellers in developing countries – wage-labourers, landless people, casual farm workers, craftspeople, petty traders etc. – in general have limited access to land and water. Their earnings are low, they have few material assets and they often have limited educational and healthcare facilities.

The level of economic development in rural areas, the services available to farmers, the level of health and education, energy resources, transport and roads can all make a difference to food security. A thriving rural economy goes hand in hand with a thriving agricultural sector. Likewise a depressed rural sector does not help local farmers. In many developing nations, the low level of rural development means that people have limited purchasing power to buy food. For farmers this can be an inhibiting factor on the amount they grow. Especially in isolated areas, far away from markets, there may be no point in growing more than their own families can eat. An improvement in the overall level of rural development, and in returns from the non-farm sector, can lead to a rise in purchasing power that in turn can lead to higher food output.

Non-farm activities complement agriculture in many areas of developing countries with millions of small farmers also engaged in those activities in order to survive. The sector 'accounts for some 44 per cent of rural employment in Asia and is growing over twice as fast as farm employment in India ... [it accounts] for 45 per cent of rural employment in Africa and for an increasing share in Latin America ... and has become increasingly important as a source of income and employment for the poor'.[1]

Exploitation of the resources of rural areas may be a vital part of the survival strategies of poorer farmers. Especially in a depressed rural economy the poor may be driven to move into the forest and collect wood to sell and earn money to buy food. This may be damaging environmentally but the poor exploit the forest in order to survive. This is especially likely to happen if people lack alternative ways of earning an income.

'To keep poor rural populations from using marginal lands, off-farm work such as cottage industries, wildlife utilisation, fisheries, village-based light industries and tourism should be developed', recommends Agenda 21, the 1992 Earth Summit declaration.[2] Such off-farm enterprises would create jobs and raise incomes in rural areas. But the problem is that in economically depressed rural areas, it is difficult to get enterprises of this kind off the ground. Outside capital may be needed but difficult to attract.

THE SERVICES NEEDED

Healthcare

The most fertile soil in the world is useless unless there are people to plant seeds and to tend and harvest crops. This is often hard work; people can only do it if they are reasonably healthy. But millions of the rural poor are handicapped by malnutrition, and are vulnerable to chronic illness and injury due to unfavourable working and living environments, including unclean water and poor sanitation facilities.

Economic recession has forced the closure or privatisation of many rural health clinics and other facilities. A farmer who is ill may have to travel further for treatment and also pay, which she/he may be unable to afford.

HIV/AIDS

One of the most serious threats to agriculture and household food security is the HIV/AIDS epidemic. An FAO report estimates that since 1985 some 7 million agricultural workers have died from AIDS-related diseases in 27 African countries. 'Throughout history, few crises have presented such a threat to human health and social and economic progress as does the HIV/AIDS epidemic', it says. This is especially the case in Africa where 25 million of the 36 million victims live.[3]

Since the disease commonly strikes the most economically productive members of society, it seriously undermines agricultural output. By 2001 the epidemic was having a major impact on agricultural production, nutrition and food security, spreading with alarming speed into the remotest villages, cutting food production and threatening the life of rural communities. As adults fall ill and die, families face declining productivity as well as loss of knowledge about indigenous farming methods and loss of assets. A downward spiral of a family's welfare often begins when the first adult in a household falls ill, with food production and income dropping dramatically as more adults are affected.

Research in Tanzania, for example, showed that per capita food consumption dropped by 15 per cent in the poorest households when an adult died. Food consumption is especially affected when mothers die as they are usually responsible for meal preparation. For the patient, malnutrition and HIV/AIDS can form a vicious cycle, with undernutrition increasing the susceptibility to infections and consequently worsening the impact of the disease.

Treating the epidemic requires increased spending from individuals on healthcare at a time of decreasing farm incomes. Once its savings are used up coping with the disease, a family might seek support from relatives, borrow money or sell its productive assets. The impact of AIDS differs from village to village and country to country, says the FAO, but it is clear that the epidemic is undermining the progress made in the last 40 years of agricultural and rural development.

Rural communities also bear a higher burden of the cost of HIV/AIDS when urban dwellers and migrant labourers return to their village of origin after falling ill. Household expenditures rise to meet medical bills and funeral expenses, at the same time as the number of productive family members declines and dependents grow. This stark position endangers both short-term and long-term household food security.

In Africa AIDS could kill 16 million more people within the next 20 years, warns the FAO. But agriculture in other developing continents is also affected. In India around four million people are infected with HIV. The incidence of the disease is high in several Caribbean countries. In Latin America the disease has been slower to spread than in other regions and is concentrated mainly in urban areas.

Biological and social factors make women and girls more vulnerable to HIV/AIDS than men and boys. It is females who face the greatest burden, having traditional responsibilities for growing and preparing food and caring for the sick. In many hard-hit communities, girls are being withdrawn from school to help lighten the family load. Studies have shown that HIV infection rates in young women can be 3–5 times higher than among young men. Also, some of the traditional mechanisms to ensure women's access to land, in case of widowhood, contribute to the spread of AIDS – such as the custom that obliges a man to marry his brother's widow.

According to the FAO report, the loss of able-bodied adults affects the entire society's ability to maintain and reproduce itself. Agricultural skills may be lost since children are unable to observe their parents working. Affected rural families often transfer to non-farm jobs. Some people migrate in search of employment or look for quick money, which may lead to such high-risk behaviour as drug abuse and prostitution.

The report advocates a review of laws and practices concerning access to land and resources to ensure that the livelihoods of widows, orphans and other poor HIV/AIDS-affected households are protected. Other recommendations include the establishment of household food security and community nutrition programmes, as well as the training of agricultural extension workers to assist affected households. The report recommends that donor countries assist in HIV/AIDS prevention and help to reduce its negative impact on food security by providing advice and resources to countries heavily

affected by the virus. Such assistance, it says, might include food aid
to provide supplementary feeding to households and orphanages.[4]

Although the situation is dire, specialists believe that the HIV/
AIDS epidemic can be brought under control. The pharmaceutical
companies are coming under pressure to make low-cost drugs available to treat the disease. Education is proving to be a powerful
weapon. In countries with strong public educational campaigns, such
as Uganda, rates of infection are coming down. In schools where
HIV/AIDS education is passed on to young people by their own
classmates, *rates of infection have dropped sixfold.*[5]

New Sources of Energy

Agriculture and its related activities require energy in one form or
another. A pump for irrigation, fuel to take produce to market, etc.,
all need power. Energy sources are often unaffordable by resource-
poor farmers (almost two billion people in developing countries do
not have access to electricity). Renewable energies such as biomass,
solar and wind, are receiving more attention, with recognition growing that they can make an important contribution to food security –
for example through irrigation, processing and conservation.

Solar systems especially have considerable potential. While these
systems have often been installed for household lighting, they could
have much wider application. Increased use of solar energy 'could
significantly improve the livelihoods of millions of people in rural
areas in developing countries', according to an FAO report, which
gives many examples of solar energy application in agriculture. But
the most disadvantaged, subsistence farmers, it cautions, 'will generally not be able to afford solar systems. Solar systems do, however,
provide some particular advantages that make them interesting for
basic social services such as water supply and vaccine refrigeration, as
well as for several niche-applications. With lower prices, the size and
number of niches will grow'.[6]

Solar photovoltaics could be used for irrigation, cattle watering,
drinking water pumping, small cottage and agro-industries, facilitating
educational radio and television programmes and health services. But

the introduction of photovoltaics faces several barriers such as high investment costs, lack of financing and infrastructure, low volumes of sales, lack of political commitment and policies. Innovative financial schemes such as revolving funds and soft loans to farmer cooperatives may be needed to open up new opportunities for the application of solar technologies.

Agriculture also has the potential to become a major energy producer. Agricultural residues can be converted into energy to the benefit of households, communities and national energy balances. This is the case with sugar bagasse in places such as the islands of Reunion, Mauritius, Hawaii and Cuba and, more recently, Nicaragua. The potential of combined production of sugar and electricity to be fed to the grid is again significant. Purposely grown biomass for energy also has high potential, especially in the context of land set-aside, land rehabilitation and reforestation programmes. But this form of energy production should not, however, enter into competition with land for food production.

ACCESS TO MARKETS

Many rural communities do not have roads or access to a road network. In the Philippines, for example, less than half the country's villages have such access, while in Bangladesh 80 per cent of villages have no direct access to mechanised means of transport. Lack of roads increases the workload of farming families. In places where goods are transported by people or animals, it is not unusual for farmers to have to travel 30 or 40 kilometres to take their produce to market.

Development agencies often stress that roads are vital if farmers are to buy agricultural inputs and take food to market. The FAO, for example, says that transport 'whether traditional or mechanised is needed to move the agricultural commodities from the harvest fields, to the threshing or drying site ... to the farmer's storehouses or to collection-centre warehouses ... to the processing industries or to bigger central storage buildings ... from these industries or storage buildings to wholesalers or retailers for final marketing'.[7]

Without roads, products are often carried in small quantities over rough tracks and footpaths. This entails long transport times and high costs per unit of product transported, leading to a squeeze on incomes. This hardly encourages farmers to increase their production. 'To alleviate these disadvantages, the road network would have to be improved to permit development of a small-scale transport system to meet the needs of the most distant production areas', says the FAO. In places where the road network is underdeveloped and agriculture is traditional, products are generally transported by people, donkeys, camels and sometimes horses.

In the last three decades of the twentieth century there was considerable investment in new roads but with generally disappointing results. Food output often did not respond in the way that had been hoped. Road improvement programmes seem to have encouraged specialised trade, such as transporting crops for export to market, rather than helping domestic food production.

> All too often people overlook the fact that roads are not an end in themselves but rather a means to an end ... what the farmer needs is effective access to a market. If the farmer lived in a village with a lively source of demand for produce and the capacity to produce the other commodities that he or she wanted, the need for long distance transport might not exist.[8]

While roads can have a positive impact on food output, again they are of no value unless the farmer has transport. Resource-poor farmers normally cannot afford motor vehicles, but a new road could make feasible some kind of transport service to meet their needs. The transport industry would require the capacity for this kind of service. Bicycles and other human-powered vehicles could play a part – a good surface can make a substantial difference. Roads to serve villages need to be well constructed but not necessarily wide or expensive.

EDUCATIONAL FEES AND FOOD SECURITY

The right to education belongs to every child but millions do not attend school, with girls especially kept away if a family's income is low or under pressure. While farming families often rely on the labour of their children in the fields, usually they prefer to send them to school. But this costs money and many will sell their food, if necessary, to raise the amount they need.

An example of this arises from the North Western Province Area Development Project in Zambia (see Chapter 10). Under the project, the province has been transformed 'into a substantial maize producer', according to an evaluation by the UN's International Fund for Agricultural Development. But although food output has increased, the incidence of malnutrition has remained as high as before the project started.

'When people grow more food, they might sell it and use some of the money to send their children to school', said a project nutritionist, 'so they do not necessarily eat more'. Following the imposition of a World Bank-IMF structural adjustment programme (SAP) on Zambia, education is no longer free (see below). The continuing high rates of malnutrition in the North Western Province are therefore linked to the policies of the international financial institutions.

Zambia is one of many countries where the imposition of a SAP has caused people to divert money away from food to education and healthcare. Parents in many countries face the acute dilemma of whether to give their children extra food to eat, and feed their bodies, or to sell food to meet school bills, and feed their children's minds. Higher food output may not lower malnutrition rates in a situation where parents choose to spend the extra money it brings on education and the greater opportunities this affords their children. The task of lessening malnutrition would be helped if there were less pressure on people to exchange food for essential services such as education.

CHAPTER 12

THE ROLE OF TRADE

Famines are caused by the grain trade.
Bertolt Brecht

India desperate to export rice.
newspaper headline

The practice and rules of international trade have a considerable impact on agriculture in developing countries. Between 1820 and 1992 income per head (globally) increased 8-fold, world income 40-fold and world trade 540-fold.[1] Foodstuffs are part of this trade, historically crossing borders because one country wants a food that it cannot produce itself – a temperate zone country cannot grow tea for example – or can only produce at a higher cost.

In the nineteenth century, the trading of foodstuffs increased with the advent of colonialism when some of the best land in Africa, Asia and Latin America was used to grow food for export to the metropolitan economies. While trade in foodstuffs grew slowly in the 30 years following World War Two, it increased rapidly in the last quarter of the twentieth century, as a result of successive rounds of trade liberalisation and the trend towards the integration of the world economy. A further reason why governments of developing countries now trade foodstuffs is that people abroad can afford to buy them, unlike most of the poor in their own countries.

WORLD FOOD PRODUCTION AND TRADE, 1968–1998

	PRODUCTION (m. tonnes)			INTERNATIONAL TRADE (m. tonnes)		
	1968	1998	% increase	1968	1998	% increase
Cereals	1064.6	1883.7	76.9	106.3	271.7	155.6
Vegetables	251.1	625.1	148.9	8.7	38.1	337.9
Vegetable oil	25.0	86.2	244.8	5.1	36.8	621.6
Fruit	223.8	430.9	92.5	21.8	81.3	272.9
Meat	94.8	222.4	134.6	5.6	23.0	310.7
Milk	389.5	557.0	43.0	25.4	69.2	172.4

Note: the trade figures are based on data for exports.

Source: FAO Food Balance Sheet Database, 2001.

For many key food products, the increase in international trade between 1968 and 1998 was over twice that of production, as the table above shows.

International trade is a controversial weapon in the battle against food insecurity; it has both raised living standards and caused people to go hungry and even starve. During Ireland's famine of 1846–47, which killed almost a million people, 'large landowners routinely exported food to Britain as poor peasants dropped all around them'.[2] But food is still today exported from countries where there is chronic hunger.

While trade has helped countries such as China, South Korea and others in east Asia to reduce malnutrition and poverty, it has done little to help most of Sub-Saharan Africa. Developing countries often export food to earn foreign exchange. Headlines such as 'India desperate to export rice' are ironic as India has over 200 million chronically hungry people who are desperate to eat more rice. The money that governments earn from exporting food is unlikely to be of any direct benefit to agriculture or to the hungry.[3]

'Without trade, countries would have to rely exclusively on their own production; overall incomes would be far lower, the choice of goods would be far less and hunger would increase', says the FAO. But it adds that the relation of trade to food security raises a number of complex issues and that the expansion in the volume of trade 'has been accompanied by declining terms of trade for the products of developing countries, which have eroded possible gains considerably'.[4]

Especially since the advent of World Bank/IMF structural adjustment programmes (SAPs) in the early 1980s, developing countries have come under pressure from donors to pay higher prices to farmers who grow crops for export, in the hope of increasing export earnings (see Chapter 3). A resource-poor country may have to choose, however, between putting scarce resources into increasing trade or into domestic agriculture. SAPs assumed that the 'adjustments' would lead to higher rates of economic growth and benefit the poor. At least in Sub-Saharan African this has not materialised.

Between 1960 and 1980, before SAPs, income per head in the region grew by a third. Between 1980 and 1997 it fell by a quarter. Part of the problem was that higher earnings from export crops did *not* come about. In mid-2001 the price of every major traded agricultural commodity, apart from sugar, was substantially lower, than, for example, in mid-1998. The world price of coffee had fallen by more than half because of oversupply, the price of palm oil by almost two-thirds. In the face of low world prices, the prices to farmers have been difficult for governments to sustain. And returns to farmers from export crops have often fallen below the cost of production, again driving many into poverty – a direct result of SAPs.

This attention to export crops has meant that more land – frequently some of the best – has been brought under such crops and that less land and fewer resources are available for domestic food crops. Export crops also tend to have higher environmental costs. They require the application of more chemicals than domestic food crops, raising questions for long-term sustainability. Around a quarter of pesticides are sprayed on cotton alone. Flying food around the world demands more fossil fuel and adds to global warming.

While trade has the potential to contribute to food security, there is now a great deal less confidence that the mainstream trading system can help the chronically hungry. Yet trade dominates the international economy. Laws and regulations which stand in its way, even if they are designed to safeguard smallholder agriculture, must be revoked. This dominance has intensified since 1995 and the coming into being of the World Trade Organisation (WTO).

THE WTO AGREEMENT ON AGRICULTURE'S IMPACT ON THE POOR

The WTO was the outcome of the Uruguay Round of trade talks held from 1986 to 1993 under the auspices of the 1947 General Agreement on Tariffs and Trade (GATT). Like the GATT, the WTO is not a United Nations agency. The Uruguay Round talks included agriculture (also services) for the first time. The Agreement on Agriculture (AoA) was one of four agreements to emerge from the talks.

The AoA is basically a pact between the US and the EU; developing countries had minimal input. It covers market access, export subsidies and domestic support for agriculture. Non-trade concerns, including food security, are mentioned in the agreement's preamble.

Under the AoA, member countries of the WTO (142 at 1 October 2001) can provide investment subsidies, input subsidies to low-income or resource-poor producers, and give support to encourage diversification from illegal narcotic crop cultivation, as long as they do not exceed the level of support given in 1993. Negative effects of the agreement are foreseen. 'Commitments ... should be made in an equitable way among all members, having regard to non-trade concerns, including food security and the need to protect the environment ... and taking into account the possible negative effects of the implementation ... on least developed and net food-importing countries'.[5]

Member countries are obliged to reduce tariffs on imported food by 36 per cent over six years (beginning in 1995) and also to convert non-tariff barriers, like quota restrictions, into tariffs — so-called 'tariffication'. For developing countries the required reduction is 24 per cent, which can be spread over ten years. Countries also had to cut export subsidies to their farmers by 36 per cent over six years; again, for developing countries the required reduction is 24 per cent, spread over ten years. Government subsidies to farmers had to be reduced by 20 per cent, 13.33 per cent in the case of developing countries. These reduction commitments did not apply to the least developed countries, although they are still subject to tariffication.

Industrialised countries who were affording high levels of protection before 1993 can continue with those levels, but developing countries cannot step up their support. WTO members are also obliged to provide 'minimum access' for agricultural produce they do not export in significant quantities – they had to import a minimum 4 per cent of their food requirements by 2000. The least developed are again exempt.

The AoA allows members to place certain policies in a 'green box'. These are exempt from reductions, as they are deemed to be non-trade distorting. They include spending on domestic food aid, public stockholding for food security purposes, safety-net programmes and disaster relief. More significant measures, such as import controls, cannot be placed in the box. The AoA also has a blue box under which direct government payments that are related to production-limiting programmes are exempt from reductions. It has a 'Peace Clause' under which member countries can take action against imports which pose a threat; this is restricted to items which can be placed in the green and blue boxes.

While WTO rules permit developing countries to place some tariffs on agricultural imports, the structural adjustment programmes of the World Bank and the IMF may prohibit them from doing so. A country's WTO commitments cannot therefore be separated from obligations to other international bodies.

The WTO's special boxes and provisions have meant little in practice. Two sets of rules have effectively been enforced under the agreement, says Rashid Kaulab of the South Centre: 'one for those who were responsible for distorting the market through tariff and non-tariff barriers and high domestic and export subsidies; they have been allowed to continue to do so with only minor adjustments.

The second set of rules is for those, including developing countries, who were not indulging in such practices. Now they are legally prohibited to do so'.[6]

In practice it is Western countries, not developing countries, that have received special treatment. The European Union and the United States have not only maintained their protectionist devices, they have sharply increased subsidies and support for their agriculture – from US$182 billion in 1995 when the WTO was set up, to $280 billion in 1997 and to $327 billion in 2000.

The 'special treatment' that developing countries were supposed to receive on processed products, including foodstuffs, is again negative. A system of tariff escalation means that higher tariffs are placed against their processed goods: the greater the processing, the higher the tariff. This hinders processing in these countries.

The evidence is that trade liberalisation has led to an influx of cheap food imports into the developing world, which is putting farmers out of business. Such imports are coming not only from developed countries (especially the US and the EU) but also from other developing nations, for example the Philippines and Thailand. They are coming in through both commercial channels and dumping – food sold below the cost of production to dispose of surpluses and usually cheaper than commercial imports. Having produced staple foods, farmers cannot obtain economic prices for them, even in village markets. Their produce cannot compete with cheaper imports. Agricultural sectors are placed in jeopardy and domestic food production is threatened.

Case studies and experiences of the effects of trade liberalisation on communities are highly consistent. 'Liberalised trade, including WTO trade agreements, benefits only the rich while the majority of the poor do not benefit but are instead made more vulnerable to food insecurity', says a study of Kenya, for example.[7]

Liberalisation has led to an increase in the prices of farm inputs, causing huge problems for small farmers. Forced to pay more for their inputs, they are often receiving less for their produce when they come to sell. Trade liberalisation appears therefore to have worsened the terms of trade between outputs and inputs.

Harvested food prices have not always fallen. In some countries – Madagascar, for example – there has been a significant rise in the price of major food crops, particularly rice. But because most of Madagascar's small farmers are net rice buyers, liberalisation 'seems to have induced significant welfare losses among the country's primarily rural poor'.[8] Higher food prices as a result of trade liberalisation would appear to be the exception.

Changes are needed in the AoA to allow developing countries to take specific measures to safeguard the livelihoods of small farmers. There could for example be a 'food security box' that permits governments of developing countries to take measures to safeguard farmers who produce staple foods. 'How can we refuse to allow others what we have had ourselves?', asks Herve Le Stum, director of the French grain producers union.[9]

How Transnational Corporations Dominate Agriculture

Their size and power give transnational corporations (TNCs) a dominant role in developing countries. Seventy per cent of international trade is between TNCs. It is corporations that trade rather than countries, and it is TNCs that have a large say in setting the terms under which they trade. They had a major influence in the talks that led up to the setting up of the WTO, both through lobbying and, especially in the case of the United States, through membership of national delegations. It some cases it was TNCs that provided the wording of agreements. Despite their influence, the activities of TNCs remain unregulated.

Nowhere is the dominance of TNCs more pronounced than in agriculture. Vertically integrated corporations now monopolise almost every aspect of farm production and distribution, from seeds, fertilisers and equipment, to processing, transporting and marketing. Four biotech companies own 44 per cent of patents on the world's most important food crops (see table p. 125). International agri-food TNCs have a 'market concentration that spans chemical fertilisers, pesticides, seeds, grain sales, livestock production, processing, shipping and retail', says Sophia Murphy of the the US-based Institute for Agriculture and Trade Policy. Governments should recognise 'how few companies are involved in this at the global level'.[10]

Six corporations account for about 85 per cent of world trade in grain, eight account for between 55 to 60 per cent of world coffee sales, seven account for 90 per cent of the tea consumed in Western countries, three account for 83 per cent of world trade in cocoa, three account for 80 per cent of bananas. Through its ownership of grain elevators, rail links, terminals and the barges and ships needed to move grain around the world, the private corporation Cargill controls 80 per cent of global grain distribution. Four other companies control 87 per cent of American beef and another four control 84 per cent of American cereal. Three agribusinesses (Syngenta, DuPont and Monsanto) account for nearly two-thirds of the global pesticide market, almost one-quarter of the global seed market and virtually 100 per cent of the transgenic seed market.[11]

The transfer of land from food crops to export crops is again aiding TNCs. An extra million hectares a year is going under plantation crops that are destined for export markets. The effects of trade liberalisation have accentuated the trend, threatening local food production and increasing the migration of people to urban areas. Livelihoods have been devastated and larger entities, including corporations, have taken over their land.

Based in Minneapolis, Cargill is one of the largest agribusiness TNCs. It describes itself as 'an international marketer, processor and distributor of agricultural, food, financial and industrial products and services with 90,000 employees in 60 countries. The company provides distinctive customer solutions in supply chain management, food applications, and health and nutrition'.[12] It is the world's largest oilseed trader, the second largest phosphate fertiliser producer and a major trader in grain, coffee, cocoa, sugar, seeds, malt and poultry. Cargill's turnover in 2000 was US$48 billion, roughly equivalent to the gross domestic products of the 28 poorest countries combined.[13] Descendants of Cargill's founder own 85 per cent of the company.

The company's activities have a direct bearing on food security. 'Cargill's corporate goal is to double every five to seven years, but the achievement of this goal requires the occupation of more and more territory, and the expulsion of whole societies from their settlements and their commons'.[14] This shows very clearly the way that TNC expansion comes at the expense of smallholders. Cargill has 'structural control of the food system, in terms of integration up and down the food chain'.[15] It has tried to convince developing countries that self-sufficiency in food output is not a practical answer to their problems. 'Expanded trade is necessary to smooth out regional supply swings and harness the productivity of low-cost producers worldwide', it claims.[16] Self-sufficiency would wrest control of the food chain away from Cargill.

Many TNCs prefer not to own land but to employ farmers on a contract basis, supplying them with inputs and advice and buying their harvested product – on the company's terms. Size and money give the corporations the power in developing countries to decide the level of prices they pay to farmers. This type of sub-contracting is common with tobacco.

TNCs favour monocropping and, wherever possible, will require farmers to buy their brand of inputs and forbid them from keeping or selling seed. By controlling germplasm from seed to sale, TNCs are moving to monopolistic control of the food chain that allows them to extract maximum profit.

The system of patents, and the corporate role in genetically modified foods, pose a potential threat to small-scale farmers and food security. Patents on plants are new in agriculture – they were originally designed for industrial innovations. But in the 1990s, TNCs began to take out patents on plant species, most of which are found in Africa, Asia and Latin America. This followed a period of intense activity when the agrochemical corporations bought up hundreds of small-scale family seed businesses. Through patenting, the TNCs seek to exploit a valuable Third World resource. They argue that they can only afford to invest large sums of money in breeding activities if their investment is protected. Patents are big business for the corporations but mean that Third World farmers have to pay them high prices for 'improved' varieties.

Traditionally, even newly developed varieties of crops such as rice have always been made freely available to all farmers. Concepts such as intellectual property rights are in danger of changing long-cherished traditions that have seen crop varieties shared freely among poor farmers.

Laws governing the inventions that can be patented vary from country to country. The United States is practically alone in allowing patents on life forms. Other countries have judged patent systems to be unsuitable for living organisms. India, for example, which has around 15,000 plant varieties unique to the country, does not allow patents to be taken out on them. The Indian Patents Act of 1970 makes it clear that inventions relating to agricultural and horticultural processes are not patentable on the grounds that socially valuable products ought not to be privatised or priced out of reach of the general public.

The WTO agreement on Trade-Related Intellectual Property Rights (TRIPs) effectively globalises the patent system. The agreement, which came into force in 1995, grants corporations the right to protect their 'intellectual property' in all member countries of the WTO. But this threatens the sovereignty of small-scale farmers. 'Patents on rice, sorghum, cassava, maize, millet, potato, soybean and wheat are falling into company hands ... This raises questions for food security'.[17]

The number of patents on five crops that account for over 70 per cent of the world's food supply is huge, and four corporations hold the lion's share, as the table below shows.

Many of the Du Pont patents were originally taken out by Pioneer Hi-Bred; the two companies merged in 1999. Syngenta was a merger in late 2000 between the agrochemical operations of AstraZeneca and Novartis. In two years, six agri-corporations have therefore merged into four, holding between them 3,955 patents on rice, maize, wheat, soybean, potato and sorghum. The total number of patents on these crops is 9,027 – which means that four giant companies hold almost 44 per cent of the patents on staple crops that are vital for the poor. In the case of soybean that figure is nearly 80 per cent, with the four TNCs holding 750 out of 947 patents. These figures

PATENT HOLDERS ON SIX LEADING STAPLE FOODS

	Rice	Maize	Wheat	Soybean	Potato	Sorghum	Total
Du Pont	191	665	539	495	3	2	1,895
Syngenta	75	198	665	21	46	15	1,020
Monsanto	80	136	290	229	32	—	767
Mitsui	267	—	1	5	—	—	273
Totals	613	999	1,495	750	81	17	3,955

Source: 'Crops and robbers', Action Aid, October 2001.

show that the food chain is falling under the control of an ever smaller number of powerful corporations.

The power of TNCs means that small-scale farmers are likely to gain few benefits from the mainstream international trade system. While greater market access to the EU and US might benefit developing countries as a whole, it would do little to help the small-scale producers. They would be competing with the far more powerful corporations. For low-income agricultural producers, 'the benefits of liberalisation ... are likely to be very limited', concludes a UN Conference on Trade and Development Report (UNCTAD) report.[18]

Alternative trade, 'fair trade', offers some hope. This is expanding rapidly, by almost 20 per cent a year and in some cases much higher. Sales of fairly traded coffee in the UK increased by 49 per cent a year, for example, between 1995 and 2000.[19] Five per cent of all coffee growers are now selling through this system and receiving more than twice as much as the world price. The trade strengthens the position of local producers and could act as a countervailing power to that of TNCs.

FOOD VERSUS EXPORT CROPS: THE RIGHT BALANCE

Land for food is scarce in developing countries (see Chapter 8) but about 15 per cent of their cultivated land is under crops being grown for export, such as coffee, cocoa, tea, sugar and, more recently, vegetables and flowers. For farmers, dependence on export crops is risky, making them vulnerable to world market-price fluctuations over which they have no control. The development of land for export crops also increases the disparities between richer and poorer farmers as only those with access to cash and credit can afford the necessary inputs.

The foreign exchange that countries earn from the export of primary crops enables governments to buy imports such as oil and other essentials. If world prices for the crops are good, then the trade makes sense for both governments and farmers. But prices of many export crops are historically very low, yielding producing countries, including the growers, only a meagre return. And it can be difficult for growers to switch to other crops. The problem for many countries is over-dependence on export crops: 25 African countries, for example, earn over 80 per cent of their foreign exchange from the sales of primary crops.

Trade liberalisation and foreign debt burdens have added to the pressure on governments to step up the production of export crops, which in turn means less land on which to grow food for local people. There is a balance to be struck between crops for local consumption and crops for export. The low level of world prices for export crops in 2001 suggests the existing balance is wrong – that there is too much land under export cultivation.

A reduction in land under export crops, and subsequently in output, could raise world prices and returns to producers; it could also release land on which food for local people could be grown. But any reduction in exports requires agreement among producing countries. And managing the supply of commodities that come onto the world market can be effective only if it is undertaken by producers accounting for the bulk of world exports.

The larger number of producing countries, the greater the difficulty in reaching agreement. But the more the price of a commodity falls, the greater the incentive for producing countries to come together and surmount the obstacles. Recent history has no examples of such collaboration.

Yet low prices could be the spur. Plans for correcting the balance are notably lacking, but one idea for producer cooperation was put forward in 1984 in a report by the Commonwealth Secretariat which is still timely. The report, 'Export Taxes on Primary Products', suggests that countries exporting primary raw materials could gain substantially by jointly agreeing to impose export taxes on their products.[20] It shows how producing countries can obtain higher revenues from their exports of primary commodities, and that it is feasible for them to act in concert, put taxes on their exports and increase their overall revenue. Seventeen primary products were examined, many of which are produced almost exclusively in developing countries.

The report looked at what might happen if countries imposed a 10 per cent, 20 per cent or 25 per cent export tax. In the consuming country, the price would rise and mean that less was purchased – but not much less, it seems, for most products. On eight of the world's largest traded commodities – coffee, cocoa, tea, bananas, bauxite, copper, tin and tropical timber – the fall in demand would be modest, and producers would gain overall, no matter which of the three rates they applied.

With a 10 per cent tax, the additional revenue from the eight products could be around US$4 billion a year, while a 25 per cent tax could bring in $10.5 billion. If sugar-producing countries could agree to impose a 25 per cent export tax, the increase in export revenue is calculated to be around 23 per cent. For cocoa, coffee and copper producers it is estimated at 13 per cent, and for tea-producing countries, 9 per cent. The report suggests that for coffee, cocoa and tea, the most advantageous export tax for producing countries to levy would be over 100 per cent.

Export taxes would be administratively simple to operate, said the report, and mean that countries would not be restricted to exporting only a certain quota of a product, as some have done under international commodity agreements. And negotiation between primary-producing and Western countries would be unnecessary. Such taxes call for substantial cooperation between developing nations.

With prices of primary commodities lower at the beginning of the third millennium than in 1984, the idea of taxes on export crops is more relevant than ever, both in terms of yielding higher earnings for farmers and governments, and increasing the land that is available for food crops. Export taxes could therefore make a contribution to a balanced pattern of agriculture, and to food security.

CHAPTER 13

ENVIRONMENTAL IMPACTS

Ecology is actually a more important science than economics –
the profitable exchange of goods within a ship is a less important matter than how to keep the whole ship above water.

Mary Midgley

Environmental factors impact heavily on agriculture, and agriculture
in turn has a big impact on the environment. The 'mining' of soil by
heavy, continuous use of chemicals and machinery can lead to dust
bowls unfit for food output, as vividly portrayed in John Steinbeck's
The Grapes of Wrath. Poorly constructed irrigation systems can lead
to serious damage (see Chapter 7). The axing of forests to make way
for plantations can change micro-climates and lead to an increase in
floods, droughts and smoke pollution. The loss of biodiversity resulting from 'modern agriculture' threatens to erode the number of
plants available to breed new varieties of crops. But agriculture and
food output are under serious threat from external environmental
changes. Global warming is probably the most serious.

GLOBAL WARMING: THE INDISPUTABLE DANGERS

There is now overwhelming evidence that human-induced greenhouse gas emissions are contributing to a warming of the climate
and to greater variability of weather patterns.

During the twentieth century, the global average temperature rose
by about 0.6°C. Atmospheric concentrations of greenhouse gases

increased by about 1 per cent a year and most of the highest yearly temperature records were concentrated in the 1990s. Three gases – carbon dioxide, nitrous oxide and methane – account for most of the emissions that cause global warming. In the twentieth century the level of carbon dioxide in the atmosphere increased by 25 per cent, nitrous oxide by 19 per cent, and methane by 100 per cent.

There is widespread agreement among scientists about the impact of climate change on agriculture. In 2001 the United Nations Inter-governmental Panel on Climate Change (IPCC) revealed evidence showing that the earth's climate is changing faster than previously thought. The scientific evidence on global warming points to a rise in temperatures of 1.4 to 6 degrees Celsius over the next century, higher than earlier predictions. A rise of this kind would result, believes the panel, in:

- Rising sea levels and more frequent occurrence of extreme weather events, such as droughts, floods, and violent storms
- Severe water stress in the arid and semi-arid land areas in south-ern Africa, the Middle East and southern Europe
- Decreased agricultural production in many tropical and subtropical countries, especially countries in Africa and Latin America
- Higher worldwide food prices as supplies fail to keep up with the demands of an increasing population
- Major changes in the productivity and composition of critical ecological systems, particularly coral reefs and forests
- Tens of millions of people at risk from flooding and landslides, driven by projected increases in rainfall intensity and, in coastal areas, rising sea levels.[1]

Even a small increase in temperature could mean a decrease in agricultural production in many developing countries, with Sub-Saharan Africa the most vulnerable. With its low per capita fossil energy use, Sub-Saharan Africa has the lowest emissions of the green-house gases that are the major cause of climate change. Yet the region (along with low-lying small island states) 'is the most vulner-able to climate change because widespread poverty limits its capabili-ties to adapt to a continuing changing climate', according to IPCC chair, Robert T. Watson. 'Particularly at risk are the arid and semi-arid regions and the grassland areas of eastern and southern Africa, and the areas already threatened by land degradation and desertification'.[2]

The findings of an FAO study confirm this, suggesting that climate change will cause severe drought conditions in parts of Africa by 2050. An additional 30 million Africans could be affected by famine by that date, 'because of the reduced inability to grow crops in large parts of Africa'.[3]

For people who are already short of food, the implications are dire. It will be the most vulnerable farmers who bear the brunt of global warming. For subsistence farmers, and especially for people who now face a shortage of food, lower yields caused by climate change could result in reduced income, malnutrition and famine.

Neither is the climate likely to change in a smooth pattern. Rather it will be erratic and unpredictable, with severe weather devastating agriculture in some years and having little impact in others. While in some areas global warming could increase water availability in water-scarce areas, and raise crop yields in some temperate and subtropical zones, it seems that in most regions the impact will be detrimental. Agriculture will also suffer from the indirect effects of climate change: pests and pathogens may increase, soil is expected to erode and degrade because of more intense rainfall patterns, and rising levels of ozone may increase air pollution damage to crops. Livestock will also suffer from rising and more extreme temperatures; there may be less forage and feed available. As a result, individual animals may produce less food for human consumption and overall herd numbers may decrease. Severe weather will cause stress to fish production systems, increasing problems for people whose food and livelihoods depend on them.

Global warming is already leading to lower rainfall in some countries and to changes in the crops that farmers grow. In Jordan, for example, diminishing rainfall is causing farmers in the south of the country to replace cereal crops such as wheat and barley, which have grown in the area for millennia, with olive trees. Rainfall in the south averages between 100–250mm a year and farmers say there has been a noticeable drop in the last ten years.

'Rainfall in this area seems to be less each year and the land has become less productive', said Jordanian farmer Mahmood Mahadin. Like most farmers in the area he does not have irrigation and his crops are dependent on rainfall. Yields of wheat, he said, are down to 800 kg a hectare. 'Climate change is making things worse because there is less rain than there used to be', said Abdelhamid Abdouli, country manager of the UN's International Fund for Agricultural Development (IFAD), which is financing a project to help farmers switch to olive trees; 'the conversion from cereals to olive trees is driven by this and by the fact that the trees need less water'.[4]

Olive trees need watering for two years after planting but can then yield well with little rain. Mahmood Mahadin believes that the olives will eventually give him a better return. But farmers are dropping their cereal crops with some reluctance. 'Farmers feel that planting trees instead of cereal crops will make Jordan more dependent on other countries in terms of importing cereals', said Anis Tarabey of Care International, 'but from a rational point of view it's a correct policy'.[5]

It is also a 'little option' policy. Farmers who can no longer make a living growing food crops have no option but to switch to alternatives, perhaps to tree crops. Their incomes are not necessarily reduced by the switch; if their return from the alternatives is good then they could be better-off. But their incomes are more dependent on factors outside their control – in the case of farming olive trees, the price of olive oil on world markets. And it means that fewer cereals are grown world worldwide. Whereas the world is not short of cooking oil (for which most olive oil is used), with global warming it could be short of food.

More extremes of weather, more erratic rainfall, more floods and droughts are also likely, leading to land degradation. If food output is to be maintained, let alone increased, agriculturalists will have to breed crops that can grow in the harsher conditions that global warming will bring. Rice, the chief staple food for millions of people, is particularly vulnerable. One estimate of rice production in Malaysia suggests that it could fall by more than 20 per cent over the next 30 years.

In densely populated, low-lying areas of countries such as Bangladesh, China, Egypt and Indonesia, there could be huge damage to crops. Most existing crop varieties cannot cope with saline conditions and agriculture could become difficult to sustain. Sea-level rises could affect fish and prawn production worldwide. Some island countries, for example in the Pacific, will be submerged if levels rise by more than a metre, while others will be affected by the flooding of fields. Salty sea water, seeping into ground water, will provide a difficult environment for crop growth.

Global warming is also leading to increases in the number of so-called 'natural disasters', such as cyclones and hurricanes. Such disasters now appear more 'human-induced' than natural and are occurring at three times the rate they did in the 1960s.[6] Disasters such as the Mozambique floods in 2000 have damaged food growing areas, causing severe disruptions in supplies.

Under the 1997 Kyoto Protocol of the Convention on Climate Change, governments made commitments to reduce emissions of greenhouse gases by 5.2 per cent by 2010, over 1990 levels, as a first step to the much larger cuts that are necessary to stop global warming. The IPCC estimates that the world needs to cut emissions of greenhouse gases by 60 per cent of 1990 levels to stabilise the climate. A cut of 5.2 per cent would merely delay global warming a fraction; it would not stop the damage. By late 2001 even this modest cut was at risk owing to the refusal of the United States to sign the Kyoto Protocol.

Agriculture is itself a source of greenhouse gases that are causing climate change: carbon dioxide from land-use change, including deforestation, from methane (ruminant digestion and rice paddies) and nitrous oxides from fertiliser use. Agriculture has the potential to reduce emissions – by promoting, for example, improved land-use systems, reforestation and bio-energy as substitutes for fossil fuels and conservation agriculture – but the larger responsibility lies with industrialised countries who emit around 80 per cent of greenhouse gases.

Global warming threatens to wipe out the hope that new ways of practising agriculture will raise food output. If Western countries

want to assist people in the developing world, they need to drasti-
cally cut their emissions of greenhouse gases. This would be bring
far greater benefits than development aid.

SOIL: THE CRADLE OF PRODUCTION

One of the most important 'environments' for agriculture and food
production, and one under threat, is the soil. While some food is
produced in high technology, soil-less culture – so-called hydroponics – the vast majority of farmers in both developed and developing
countries grow their crops in soil. Soil is the cradle of production;
when soil goes, so also goes the means to produce food.[7]

Soils are composed of: mineral particles derived from rocks by
weathering; organic materials; humus from dead and decaying plant
material, in which nutrient elements are dissolved; carbon dioxide,
oxygen and living organisms, including bacteria, that help plant
decomposition. Under most conditions, soil is formed at a rate of 1
inch every 250–1,200 years. In all, it usually takes 3,000–12,000 years
to make agriculturally productive land. And soil is a non-renewable
resource. Once destroyed, it is practically gone forever. But soil can
be cared for and its fertility maintained.

It is however being lost and degraded at a disturbing rate. FAO
estimates suggest that the planet is currently losing up to around 7
million hectares, an area almost the size of Ireland, of cultivated land
a year due to soil degradation. If the process is not halted, it would
negate all agricultural gains from the opening of new lands to farming and pasture over the next 20 years. About 25 billion tonnes of
soil are also being washed away each year, going first into the world's
rivers and then into the oceans.

Another 910 million hectares of once-rich land, an area larger
than Australia, has become moderately degraded, which means that
it has suffered a decline in productivity. If no restoration is undertaken on such land, it may soon be strongly degraded. Neither is the
situation improving. In 1992 the FAO forecast that, over the next 20
years, up to 140 million hectares of fertile land is expected to lose
much of its agricultural value.

Overgrazing is the most prevalent cause of soil damage, responsible for 35 per cent of all erosion; continual trampling by herds compacts the soil and reduces its capacity to retain moisture. Destructive agricultural practices and mismanagement of land account for 27 per cent of soil damage. These include such practices as repeated conventional tillage with heavy equipment and mismanagement such as steep land being cultivated down the slope. When soil is compacted it is difficult to return it to full productivity.

Water erosion is also one of the most common forms of erosion, causing massive damage in nearly all developing countries. It is especially prevalent where steep land is being unwisely farmed and where gently sloping land is left exposed to the effects of heavy rain for any length of time. China's Huang River, the most sediment-laden river in the world, annually carries away 1.6 billion tonnes of soil into the East China Sea. During a short storm in Tanzania a few years ago, scientists found that a field they were studying lost 5 cm of topsoil over its whole surface in just a few hours.

Wind erosion is another cause of degradation and eventual desertification; it occurs when soil is left bare of vegetation to block the wind. It is particularly severe in arid and semi-arid areas following overstocking and overgrazing, with 22.4 per cent of Africa north of the Equator and 35.5 per cent of the Near East affected by it. Under the worst conditions, 60 tonnes of soil can be blown off one acre of land in an hour (150 tonnes a hectare).

'Soil fertility' refers to the ability of the soil be productive, 'to supply essential plant nutrients and soil water in adequate amounts and proportions for plant growth and reproduction in the absence of toxic substances which may inhibit plant growth'.[8]

Even the better soils of many parts of developing countries are becoming less productive, says the FAO, with declining fertility in areas where there is an urgent need for production increases. The main reason for this is the continuous mining of plant nutrients without adequate replenishment. Fertility is lowered when soils are deprived of their essential fertilisers and organic matter. Crop rotation and good farming practices can prevent the problem.

Maintaining soil fertility is vital if food is to be produced on a sustainable basis. The soil itself needs feeding. Chemical fertiliser is costly for small-scale farmers and can damage the long-term health of the soil. The application of chemical fertilisers can make some soil more acidic, others more saline. 'The devil's salt' is how some small farmers in Ghana, for example, have come to describe such fertilisers. 'Minimal use of chemicals preserves the organic richness of the soil and the food chain that depends on it'.[9]

Preferable and more affordable, organic fertilisers take a number of forms, including animal waste, the use of crop residues and green manures. In the latter techniques, crops are grown as 'cover crops'. Lying low to the ground they add nitrogen to the soil and also cover – suppress – weeds. In parts of Africa the cover crop mucuna is used to boost soil fertility and yields; it also helps to control soil erosion and to improve the 'physical, chemical and biological properties of the soil'.[10] Trees can also be planted to help restore soil fertility. Fast-growing, nitrogen-fixing trees have been planted in many developing countries, with the annual fall of leaves providing nitrogen to the soil.

No Food Security without Soil Security

The intensification of agriculture has led to land degradation, erosion, waterlogging and salinisation. All these are visible. Less visible, says the UN Food and Agriculture Organisation, 'are the imbalances and deficiencies in the soil's physical, chemical and biological conditions which were caused by the use of high yield varieties in monocultures and machinery and the indiscriminate applications of agrochemicals. These can be held responsible at least in part for the yield plateaus and declines now observed in farmers' fields where high-input agriculture had previously been successful.

In the areas of marginal agriculture and animal production where the Green Revolution has not penetrated, the quality of the soil largely influenced the availability of water and nutrients to the plant. The development and maintenance of soil conditions favourable to moisture storage, plant nutrition and health are even more critical because the soils are generally poor and fragile, prone to rapid degradation – a major cause of food insecurity in these areas.

Improving soil management requires a quite different approach to that of the use of the Green Revolution inputs. Soil conservation practices are often difficult to demonstrate and validate; they always need to be adapted to the local conditions of the farmer's field, and changed with the season and the weather. They are often labour-intensive, and their impact is less visible as they result merely in maintaining or slowly improving yields, and therefore they tend to be neglected by the farmer for more immediate economic returns.

There is, however, a vast array of knowledge and experience which is now available to promote more efficient soil management and conservation:

• Analyses of the extent and cost of land degradation – loss of soil fertility and erosion – at both country and global levels have been conducted.
• Figures for both agricultural productivity loss and land-improving investments are few but becoming available in both developed and developing countries.
• The World Overview of Conservation Approaches and Technologies (WOCAT) provides since 1992 a database to evaluate conservation methodologies over a wide range of environmental and social circumstances.

Soil conservation strategies are also evolving and attempt to give priority to soil productivity and farmer's income rather than considering prevention of soil erosion and soil loss as an end in itself. The soil management-cum-productivity approach enlists the participation of farmers in identifying and applying the most appropriate practices for the husbandry of their land – as they do for their crops and animals. Soil conservation then becomes an integral part of agricultural development and land care and can be promoted in any type of farm system – from traditional to commercial. In order for soil management and conservation needs to be integrated into sustainable agricultural strategies for food security, they also must be addressed at the policy, legal and institutional levels.

Ultimately the conservation and management of soil resources are matters of national interest and food security which cannot be left to the farmers alone. Governments must play a positive role. Technical support and credit facilities should help the farmers in adopting improved soil management practices and carrying out land rehabilitation and improvement works. In addition, local communities and the society at large should accept to bear part of the costs of maintaining a secure soil resources base for the food supplies to present and future generations, in particular those of major investment works in agricultural land resources reclamation and protection'.

Source: FAO Fact Sheet 2, October 2000.

DESERTIFICATION: ANOTHER THREAT

Linked to poor soils is desertification or land degradation. This is estimated to be driving around three million people a year from their rural homes and into towns and cities because their land can no longer support them. Living in dryland areas, often on the fringes of deserts, they are overwhelmingly among the world's poorest people. Almost one in six of the world's population are affected, some 900 million people.

More than 100 countries, covering some 3,600 million hectares, are seriously affected by desertification, according to FAO estimates. 'Desertification is like a "disease of the earth" which seriously affects the vegetative cover of croplands, pastures and woodlands. It has negative impacts on biological diversity, soil fertility, the hydrological cycle, crop yields and livestock production'.[11]

Desertification results from a number of factors including increasing pressure on land, climatic variations and human activities, such as overgrazing of livestock and excessive firewood cutting. When their land becomes barren and unable to produce food, the poor have no option but to move on. The Sahel region of Africa, which is home to some of the world's poorest people, is particularly affected. Lying south of the Sahara desert, the region stretches from Mauritania on the Atlantic Ocean to Ethiopia on the Red Sea. Many millions of people from the Sahel have become 'land refugees' in the last 20 years, and been forced to move south towards the West African coastline. People forced off their land may go to other rural areas which in turn can put those areas at risk of degradation.

Although poor people in marginal environments have often developed the capacity to cope with food shortages, coping systems are beginning to break down, with successive droughts pushing communities into a downhill spiral. In Burkina Faso, for example, people have migrated from the country's degraded central plateau to the humid south, causing serious tensions and putting additional strains on already over-stretched services and resources. Africa north of the Sahara is also affected with desertification, a severe problem for countries such as Algeria and Morocco.

Many farmers in India have been forced by inhospitable land to move from western Rajasthan and eastern parts of the country to neighbouring Haryana and Madhya Pradesh. Some of them have made their way to Madras, causing pressure on basic services such as water supplies. The huge growth of cities in Latin America is partly due to the influx of farmers whose land could no longer yield them a living.

Combating desertification is complex and has actively to involve local communities in decision-making processes. In some areas the problems are being successfully tackled. Clusters of trees – for example, so called 'shelterbelts' – are appearing in parts of the Sahel to shelter food-growing land from the desert. But some farmers are reluctant to invest in such measures because they do not have secure tenure to the land they farm.[12]

In 1994 the United Nations launched the Convention to Combat Desertification (UNCCD). This became operational in November 1997 and has been ratified by more than 180 countries. But only a few have implemented substantial programmes to tackle the problems.

MONOCULTURE: WHY SO DANGEROUS?

A diverse variety of plants, both wild and cultivated, is essential if crops are to be developed that yield more, resist pests and disease, and tolerate harsh environments. This diversity is an essential link in the food chain – it is the base for increased productivity as it gives humankind the capacity to adapt and develop crops for the future. Yet diversity is declining chiefly because of the replacement of local crop varieties, a direct result of green revolution technology and monoculture.

Humankind has now become dangerously dependent on a small number of crops. 'The genetic diversity of our critical plant species is disappearing at a terrible pace', says a report by the Crucible Group, made up of experts from rich and poor countries.[13] Over the last 100 years, around three-quarters of the world's known plant species have been lost, and 70 per cent of existing tropical plants could become extinct in the next 20 to 30 years.

A wide variety of plant genetic materials proved invaluable when, for example, the Indian rice crop was devastated in the 1970s by the Tungro virus. Scientists then looked at 17,000 varieties of rice 'before eventually finding resistance in a single wild variety'.[14] If a wide range of plant species is not available, farmers and scientists will be denied the material they need – and without it, humanity could face chaos, increasingly dependent on a tiny number of crops. Such over-dependence has already proved deadly.

The Irish famine in the nineteenth century occurred largely because the limited number of potato varieties planted in Ireland were all vulnerable to the same blight. More recently, blights on maize in the USA and a virus on rice in the Philippines occurred because of over-reliance on a few varieties.

Little more than 150 plant species are now under commercial cultivation; 20 crops provide 90 per cent of the world's food. Four of them – rice, maize, wheat and potato – provide well over half. Farmers in India once harvested 30,000 varieties of rice. Today, over three-quarters of India's rice crop comes from 10 varieties. In India's Green Revolution state of Punjab it is no longer possible to buy a single traditional variety of seed.

In the Philippines, 90 per cent of all the rice is sown to two varieties. In Zimbabwe, two maize varieties account for 90 per cent of the maize planted and have displaced many traditional varieties of millet and sorghum. In cases like these, should one variety be hit by a severe disease, the food security of a country could be plunged into turmoil. Such a narrow base makes food supplies highly vulnerable. A wide range of plant material is needed to reduce such vulnerability. For millions of the poor, plant diversity is a vital meal ticket.

DEFORESTATION

Between 1980 and 1990, deforestation of tropical forests was taking place at the rate of 15.5 million hectares per year. In the 1990s, according to the FAO, this decreased by about 10 per cent; but about 14 million hectares were still being lost.[15]

Forests act like a sponge, soaking up rainwater and releasing it gradually to surrounding land. When forests go, this regulation goes and agriculture can suffer from the increased incidence of both droughts and floods. The global climate has also been affected by forest loss. The main causes of the deforestation are the expansion of agriculture in Africa and Asia, large economic development programmes involving resettlement, agriculture and infrastructure in Latin America and Asia, over-harvesting of industrial wood and fuelwood, and the logging of trees for export in order to increase foreign exchange earnings. The requirements of World Bank/IMF structural adjustment programmes have intensified the pressure on governments of developing countries to log forests for export.

Some forest is cleared by landless people who are desperate for land on which to grow food. 'They moved from forest margins to escape from poverty elsewhere and they deforest in order to survive. Deforestation is not likely to slow until these people can earn a living and meet their food needs'.[16]

But it is commercial interests that have also caused forests to be cleared, often for the flimsiest, short-term purposes. Forest in the Philippines has been cleared, for example, by Japanese companies in order to turn into chop-sticks for short-term use. In the case of the Amazonian forest in Brazil, land has been cleared of trees, sometime illegally, in order to use land for cattle ranching – with the cattle destined for fast food chains. 'The burning and illegal logging [of the Amazon] is needless. The cash, technology and public concern are all there to prevent it'.[17] The cleared land may only supply ranching for a limited number of years.

Valuable forests have thus been damaged for commercial reasons and without taking into account the true cost, in terms of the harm done both to local and global environments.

In some countries natural forests and crop land have been replaced by plantations, again with the aim of earning more foreign exchange. In Indonesia, for example, forest plantations covered around 3.8 million hectares of the country in 1994. Within four years, by 1998, this had more than doubled. Plantations under palm oil grew from 600,000 hectares to over 2 million hectares in the 1990s. By 2005 the government planned to increase this to 5.5 million hectares – an almost tenfold increase of land under palm oil in 15 years. Most would be exported for use as cooking oil. But the effect on the world price of palm oil could be dire. In late September 2001 the price was £285 a tonne, less than half of the price only three years earlier.

A further aspect of tropical forests is that millions depend on them for food. The forests of Central Africa's Congo Basin, for example, serve as a rich pantry for around 24 million people who live in and around them in Cameroon, Central African Republic, Congo, Congo DR, Equatorial Guinea and Gabon. But this forest is being damaged by heavy logging of valuable trees. The logging reduces the availability of natural foods for local people and threatens to diminish the area of land they can cultivate. Forests are a vital part of the food chain. Deforestation inevitably weakens the link and is a threat to food security.

CHAPTER 14

LIVESTOCK CONNECTIONS

> Probably more people are directly involved in chicken production throughout the world than in any other single agricultural enterprise.
>
> *John Bishop, poultry specialist*

Livestock are an integral part of the farming systems of millions of resource-poor farmers. Livestock products, however, are often a luxury that are enjoyed only by better-off people. Nonetheless, in some developing countries, China for example, demand for products such as beef and poultry is rising (in contrast to Western countries where demand for red meat is declining).

In Western countries many livestock are reared in intensive-production 'battery-cage' systems, rarely seeing any grass. Among large-scale farmers in developing nations, the battery-cage system is also widespread. This type of system is controversial, with animal rights campaigners pointing to the animal cruelty involved, which sometimes manifests itself in outbreaks of disease. The ever-present likelihood of disease, plus growing political clamour for the banning of battery-cage poultry farming, puts a question mark over the sustainability of such systems.

Small-scale farmers in the developing world can rarely afford intensive systems; free-range farm animals, therefore, continue to be an important feature of their agriculture. The FAO estimates that around 2 billion people depend at least partly on farm animals for their livelihood. If they are unable to afford to eat animal products, they trade them for staple foods. Farm animal production is important for food production, manure for fertiliser and cooking, draught power, fibre, hides and leather for clothing.

'In Asian and some African semi-arid regions, livestock are integrated into smallholder and labourer livelihood systems, providing draught power and manure for cropping'.[1] Livestock are also viewed by small farmers in many countries as 'money in the bank', available to be sold in lean times or when there is a need for cash. The FAO database of farm animals lists 6,500 breeds of domesticated mammals and birds, including cattle, goats, sheep, buffalo, yaks, pigs, horses, rabbits, chickens, turkeys, ducks and geese. Cattle are 'more numerous in Asia than any other continent and about half of Asian cattle are found in India ... Ethiopia is the African country with most cattle, closely followed by Nigeria'.[2]

A mix of livestock and cropland often brings more income than either activity alone, because of the support that each can give to the other. In particular, livestock play a vital role in providing manure that can help crop growth; one tonne of cow dung, for example, 'is estimated to contain about 8 kg of nitrogen and 4 kg of potash. Also the organic content of manure helps maintain the structure, water retention and drainage capacity of the soil'.[3]

Small ruminants, sheep and goats, are popular with millions of small-scale farmers as the animals can survive on coarse feeds and scrub vegetation. Both sheep and goats number over 500 million worldwide. Goats can survive on resources that are of limited value for sheep and cattle grazing. In the hostile arid conditions of India's Thar desert, the Parbat Sagar goat might receive water only twice a week, for example, but thrives without any adverse affect on body weight. However, the browsing habits of goats have been blamed for damage to crop land and for soil degradation in arid areas.

Chickens are again popular with many small-scale farmers. Chickens running around a homestead can fertilise a homestead's soil with nutrient-rich manure, helping to raise its productivity. They can scavenge plants and food residues around farms, so reducing the need for outside inputs. Farmers value chickens for their 'adaptability, contributions to the family income and nutrition and for insect control and fertilizers ... With minimum care they can hatch and raise chicks, produce high-value meat and give eggs which meet a strategic nutritional need of children. Live chickens sold for meat bring a good price and are a primary source of household income'.[4]

Bees are small insects with huge potential for smallholders. Bees can mean both higher incomes and more food. Beekeeping requires a minimum of land and can be carried out in fields, forest and backyards. Bees produce honey and beeswax which can fetch good prices. They also pollinate crops with impressive results. According to a UN Development Programme estimate, when farmers combine beekeeping with crop farming, 'yields increase by 20 to 50 per cent'.[5]

ANIMAL TRACTION

Animal traction for tillage was introduced into developing countries during the colonial era. In the 1960s and early 1970s it received little attention from the governments of most newly independent countries. But the sharp rise in oil prices in 1973 led to a rethink. Livestock now play a valuable role in a number of traction purposes, providing important low-cost power. Buffaloes, camels, cattle, donkeys, mules, horses, oxen and other animals pull ploughs, transport produce to market and help raise water. They are also used for milling, logging, land-levelling and road construction. The type of traction is relatively affordable, requiring few external inputs. 'Work animals can be used to reduce drudgery and intensify agricultural production so raising living standards throughout rural communities'.[6]

In Ethiopia, which has the highest population of draft animals in Africa, traditional cropping systems normally involve the use of the wooden 'maresha' and plough, pulled by work oxen. Pack donkeys and mules are also widely used. In eastern and southern Africa, animal traction technology is used by around 40 per cent of farmers, varying from 5 per cent in parts of Tanzania to 95 per cent in smallholder systems in Botswana and southern Zambia.

Of particular importance is the potential of animal traction to increase crop production and food output. This type of traction can

enable resource-poor farmers to expand the area they plough, especially in larger countries, where landholdings are relatively large and
land can remain unused. But the expense of buying the technology
can be an inhibiting factor, and government support is often lacking.
'If governments proclaim support for animal traction, this is often
limited to lip service rather than to actual support in terms of credit,
extension, veterinary services etc'.[7] With fuel and other energy prices
likely to continue beyond the reach of many farmers, animal traction
has a significant role to play.

ANIMAL SPECIES IN DECLINE

While livestock is important in the agriculture of developing
countries, diversity is under threat. Every week the world loses two
breeds of its valuable domestic animal diversity, according to the
FAO. 'In the past 100 years we have already lost about 1,000 breeds',
says Keith Hammond of FAO's Animal Genetic Resources Group;
'alarmingly, without adequate action, a large number of domestic
animal breeds at risk of extinction (2,255 breeds) could be lost within
the next two decades ... Domestic animal diversity is unique and
cannot be replaced; it is not possible to replace lost diversity. Loss of
diversity is forever'.[8]

The greatest threat to domestic animal diversity is the export of
animals from developed to developing countries, says Hammond,
which leads to cross-breeding or even replacement of local breeds.
In developing countries, breeds from industrialised countries are still
considered as more productive. The problem, however, is that these
animals are mainly suited to the conditions of the country they
come from and they have difficulty coping with the often harsher
environments of the industrialising world.

The trend in Sub-Saharan Africa is particularly alarming, with the
number of mammalian breeds at risk of extinction increasing from 8
to 19 per cent between 1995 and 1999. The situation with bird
breeds is even more serious with the percentage at risk increasing
from 20 per cent in 1995 to 34 per cent in 1999. One Africa breed

at risk is the Renitelo cattle in Madagascar. This is particularly well adapted to the different climate zones in Madagascar and provides meat and draught power. But it is now nearly extinct.

The Asia and Pacific region contains more than one-fifth of the world's animal genetic resources, with 1,251 domestic animal breeds recorded. The majority of the world's buffaloes and yaks, almost half of its Muscovy ducks, pheasants and partridges, one-third of its pig breeds and one-quarter of its goat breeds are found in the region. Of the 1,251 breeds recorded, around 10 per cent are at risk. In Latin America, around 20 per cent of breeds on file are considered at risk; the total proportion of bird breeds at risk of being lost increased dramatically from five per cent in 1995 to 45 per cent in 1999.[9]

THE MEAT PROBLEM

Livestock in Western and more prosperous developing countries are often fattened on grain. This has implications for food security as rising demand for grain to feed livestock inevitably increases its price on world markets to the detriment of net food importing countries – about three-quarters of all developing countries – and food security.

Producing meat through livestock fed on grain is an inefficient use of resources. It takes several pounds of grain to produce 1 lb of pork, poultry or beef. In the 1990s Lester Brown of the Worldwatch Institute raised concerns that rising demand for beef in China would cause the country to become a huge importer of grain. Brown describes as 'startling' the way that China has overtaken the United States in its consumption per person of basic goods such as pork and eggs. 'As incomes continue to rise in China so too will grain consumption per person'.[10]

If per capita consumption of beef in China, 'currently only 4 kilograms a year, were to match that in the United States (45 kilograms) the Chinese would eat an additional 49 million tonnes of beef each year. Produced in feedlots this would take some 343 million tonnes of grain, equal to the entire US grain harvest'.[11] Such a demand would represent about a quarter of the entire global grain harvest and could lead to a sharp increase in world grain price and possibly to global food shortages.

But there are different interpretations of China's position. 'Although China's demand for grain will continue to grow and imports will rise to historic highs, increased domestic production will prevent China from bankrupting world food supplies', finds a report by one of the CGIAR centres, the International Food Policy Research Institute (IFPRI). China's domestic production of grain will rise, projects the study, from 426 million tonnes in 2000 to 570 million tonnes by 2020. The country's grain imports will be much the same in 2020 as they were in 2000, it predicts, around 25 million tonnes, and under 'a scenario of high population growth' would not reach 52 millions tonnes – 'not drastic enough to cause a global food shortage'.[12]

But China is not the only developing country where living standards will hopefully rise. Globally this will lead to higher demand for meat, and for grain to produce that meat, given current production methods. This has led to a debate on whether by the mid-twenty-first century, when the world's population seems likely to have risen from 6 billion to between 8.5 and 9 billion, the world can grow enough grain for meat production, or whether vegetarianism or low-meat diets should be encouraged. 'If the world's affluent cut their consumption of grain-fed livestock products by 10 per cent, they could free up to 64 tonnes of grain for direct human consumption'.[13]

This would clearly make a contribution to moderating world grain prices and to food security. While many people in Western countries are eating less meat because of BSE, and fears about intensive farming practices, there remains a general lack of awareness about the health risks that are associated with the excessive consumption of fat-rich livestock products. Governments of Western countries could seize the initiative and explain the risks to their publics. A tax on livestock products could also be considered. Making meat dearer would again be a contribution to moderating world grain prices.

There are also animal welfare concerns. Proponents argue that the world can produce enough food without devoting enormous resources to the production of meat, often subjecting animals to appalling treatment.[14]

OVERFISHING

Fish play an important role in the diets of many people in developing countries, accounting, for example, for around 30 per cent of the animal protein consumed by Asians and nearly 20 per cent by Africans. High in protein, it is an excellent source of minerals such as calcium, phosphorus and iron, vitamins such as A, B1, B2 and D, and it complements the high carbohydrate diets in many regions. Fish is a key part of the diets of malnourished children whose small stomachs prevent them from consuming the bulk they need to get enough nutrients. But overfishing is causing the decline of stocks and stagnation in world catches. With Westerners eating more fish − and with the purchasing power to buy it − there is progressively less fish for the people who most need it.

Global fish catches increased fivefold between 1950 and 1989, rising from around 20 million tonnes to just over 100 million tonnes. Having reached the 100 million tonne mark, the tide turned and the global catch stagnated for several years. It began to rise again from the mid-1990s but with a lower proportion of the catch coming from the seas. Inland waters, including fish farming (aquaculture) accounted for most of the increase. Of the 1999 total fish catch of 128 million tonnes, the sea catch was 78 million − down from 86.3 million tonnes in 1998.[15] Just over three-fifths of the catch was netted in developing countries. The world's largest fish producer, China, produced 38 million tonnes in 1998 − up from 17.6 million tonnes in 1993 − most of which came from aquaculture.[16] About 70 per cent of the global catch is eaten directly, and some 30 per cent is used as feed, chiefly in aquaculture and to fatten livestock.

The quality of the fish catch is declining. Less is being caught of some of the major ocean species, like Indian Ocean shrimp, Atlantic cod, bluefish tuna and halibut; these are seriously overfished. Catches of high value fish such as Atlantic cod, Cape hake and silver hake dropped from 5 million tonnes in 1970 to 2.6 in 1989. Catches of Pacific Ocean perch, Atlantic herring, Atlantic mackerel, yellow croaker and atka mackerel have all declined due to overfishing.

Fisheries are marked by overcapacity, of too many boats chasing not enough fish. The FAO recorded a doubling in the world fishing fleet between 1970 and 1990 – from 585,000 to 1,200,000 boats. Overall there are probably around 3 million fishing vessels, Using advanced technology, such as sensing systems to detect the location of fish, trawlers with nets the size of football pitches can vacuum clean the seabed. The most heavily overfished seas are the Gulf of Thailand, seas in Southeast Asia, the southern part of the North Sea and the northern Mediterranean.

Small-scale fishermen and women provide most of the seafood consumed by local populations, yet they number among the poorest of the poor. Around 200 million fishworkers in developing countries depend both directly and indirectly on fishing for their livelihoods. 'The majority of these men, women and children earn their living from fishery-related activities in small-scale, traditional or artisanal fishing communities. The characteristics and relative importance of these communities may vary across countries, but at least two aspects are universal:

- Small-scale fishing communities tend to be critically dependent on fishery resources for their food and livelihood security, and are therefore highly vulnerable to external pressures
- Small-scale fishing communities are highly dynamic, providing significant direct and indirect employment, and making important forward and backward linkages with the local economy'.[17]

Overfishing by trawlers is cutting the jobs and incomes of small-scale fishermen, impoverishing coastal communities and making it harder for the poor to afford fish. Traditional ways of life, which for centuries have been sustained by fisheries, are in danger of collapsing. Coastal fishworkers who cannot afford motors for their boats are effectively restricted to within a mile or so of the shore. With an outboard engine, they normally fish within a few miles of the coastline. Their fishing grounds can be affected by larger trawlers overfishing waters that are just outside the small fishermen's range. Spawning and feeding grounds are damaged and fewer fish flow into the shore areas.

Damage to their near-shore fishing grounds has caused many fishers to push out further from their shores in order to make a living. But their boats are not designed for deeper, rougher waters and their lives have become even more precarious. Throughout the developing world, artisanal fishermen have become aware that as fish become scarcer, there is more chance of conflict between them and large-scale industrial fishing.

Fish is unique among Third World food exports – no other nutritious food is exported in such large quantities from poor countries to rich. Fish has now become one of the developing world's chief food exports with many countries exporting an increasing percentage of their catch. 'Fish has a habit of jumping onto the tables of rich people', says Pierre Gillet of the Brussels office of the International Collective in Support of Fishworkers.[18] Such 'jumping' is possible because of trade. Exports of fishery products by developing countries were more than US$29,000 million in 1977.[19] This meant that fish earned more foreign exchange for the Third World than any other primary commodity. Coastal developing countries, especially, view the sea as a promising source of export revenue. But while the exports earn foreign exchange, they mean that less fish is available for people in low-income exporting countries. The fish trade has put certain species out of reach of local people, and protein consumption is declining as a result.

Overfishing in the waters of many Western countries is now acute. Facing increased demand for fish from their own populations, and overfished seas off their coasts, Northern countries have looked South, and made deals with Third World countries to allow them to fish in their waters. Sometimes vessels fish pirate-style in these waters without an agreement. Having stripped their own waters of fish, European boats are in danger of doing the same in the waters of the developing world. 'Greed in the North is robbing the South of the means to meet its needs', believes the Coalition for Fair Fishing Agreements (CFFA) which comprises 15 European non-governmental organisations.[20]

Open access to the seas by trawlers has been a disaster for fish stocks and for the Third World. Unless management improves, the major ocean fishing grounds could be turned into a desert with appalling consequences. A knock-on effect might unravel the oceans' entire ecosystems. 'If managed and regulated appropriately, they [fish resources] have the capacity to renew themselves and benefit people for generations to come', believes Brian O'Riordan; better management 'could yield another 20 million tonnes of fish a year'.[21]

The only way to control overfishing is to limit access to fishing grounds. This is vital if fish catches are to be sustainable. Subsidies for large-scale trawlers must be reduced by governments of both rich and poor nations. A global quota system should be considered; Australia and New Zealand have both introduced quota schemes. Regulations to control overfishing are vital, but not enough. 'If regulation is to work, it must be supported by effective surveillance and heavy penalties', believes John Beddington of Imperial College, London.[22] Poorer developing countries, especially, may need help with purchasing surveillance equipment.

Small-scale fishermen and women need to be able to participate in decisions that affect them – about resource management, appropriate technology, the type of training they need and the role of the local community. Unless there is such involvement, management schemes are unlikely to work.

CHAPTER 15

OFFICIAL AGENCIES

Our Dream is a World Free of Poverty
World Bank website

Many thousands of non-governmental organisations in both developing and developed countries are working with small-scale farmers to
eliminate hunger. Some of their work has featured in this book (see
especially Chapter 5). A number of intergovernmental development
agencies, with far greater financial resources, share NGO goals, at
least in theory. The rhetoric of some of the major official agencies,
however, frequently runs ahead of performance; their achievements
are often limited and some of their policies may even worsen the
poverty they 'dream' of defeating.

WORLD BANK: THE RECORD

Set up at Bretton Woods in the USA in 1945, the World Bank is the
world's largest multilateral aid organisation and probably its most
controversial – not just for the money it lends to developing countries
but for the influence it yields and the advice it gives. The Bank's
total lending in 2000 amounted to US$15.3 billion[1] which is almost
a third of the world's development aid. Spread over its 180 member
countries, however, its loans are comparatively modest, although large
compared with those of the NGOs.

In return for its modest loans and grants, the World Bank hands out advice to a recipient country on how to run its economy. It expects the advice to be taken and effectively has developing countries over a barrel. The Bank sends economic advisors who 'recommend' countries to adjust their economies in line with free-market economy theory, on pain of receiving no more aid, debt relief or investment. This has led to the charge, even from free marketeers, that the Bank and its sister organisation, the International Monetary Fund, act in a neocolonialist fashion. 'They sit in judgement on governments, using their financial clout to influence economic policy in scores of developing countries'.[2]

The World Bank's huge influence cannot hide its dismal record on agricultural and related issues. When, for example, the world price of coffee slumped in mid-2001 close to its lowest levels for 30 years, analysts put the blame on the huge surplus of the supply of coffee over demand. The reason for the big increase in supply was that Vietnam had come from practically nowhere to become the world's second largest coffee-producing country after Brazil. And Vietnam had done it with World Bank support.

In the early 1990s Vietnam's farmers were constrained from diversifying into export crops like coffee because of lack of money to buy inputs, and the difficulty they had obtaining credit. The World Bank made a loan for restructuring the agricultural sector with about half of it going to rural credit programmes (see Chapter 10 for details).

The world coffee market could not cope with the extra coffee that was produced. In 2000 the world price halved, to the distress of farmers who grow coffee in over 70 countries. It continued to fall in 2001. Vietnam is far from the only county where the World Bank has supported coffee production. Poor farmers throughout the world, who grow coffee as a cash crop, are being hit by the Bank's loans. The Bank's website in 2001 listed 22 projects related to coffee: Nicaragua, Mexico, Uganda, Côte d'Ivoire, El Salvador, Indonesia, Burundi, Kenya, Togo, Zambia, Equatorial Guinea, Ethiopia, Dominican Republic and Rwanda all received World Bank support.

The Bank employs highly paid and seemingly well-qualified economists. But by taking a country-by-country approach it appears blind to what every undergraduate student of economics knows: if producing countries across the board are being assisted to increase their output at a time when world demand is sluggish, the end result can only be a fall in prices. And this fall increases the smallholder poverty that the World Bank 'dreams' of defeating. The tragic irony is that such encouragement of additional export crop production is being done with scarce aid money.

Neither is coffee the only export crop that has received support from the World Bank. Cocoa is another commodity characterised by oversupply and low prices. The Bank's support for cocoa includes the Private Sector Development in Coffee and Cocoa Trade Project in Côte d'Ivoire, the Cocoa Rehabilitation Project in Cameroon, several projects in Ghana and in Equatorial Guinea and the Dominican Republic.

The encouragement of export crops is just one of the controversial sectors in which the World Bank has become entangled. One of the most controversial is its support for large dams (see also Chapter 7). About 35,000 large dams have been built since 1950, usually creating huge reservoirs which have flooded millions of hectares of fertile land, thus affecting food output. Many of the largest schemes have been made possible only by funding from the World Bank. In total the Bank has lent over US$115 billion for more than 1,530 dam projects in over 90 countries.[3]

Bank funding has gone, for example, to China's Three Gorges Dam, to dams on Chile's Biobio River, on India's Narmada River, the Ilisu Dam in Turkey, Pak Mun Dam in Thailand, the Akosombo Dam in Ghana, Bujagali Dam in Uganda, and dams in the Lesotho Highlands Water Project. Millions of the world's poorest and most vulnerable people have been forced out of their homes as a result. The Three Gorges will displace 1.1 million people and India's Narmada Dam 250,000 people. And those affected are often not even consulted. 'People affected are often last to be told of projects that will affect their communities'.[4]

A 1997 Bank report, 'The World Bank's Experience with Large Dams: a Preliminary Review of Impacts', glossed over the negative effects of dams, allege critics.[5] The report of the World Commission on Dams revealed the true picture: 'large dams ... did not recover their costs and have been less profitable in economic terms than expected ... have a marked tendency towards schedule delays and significant costs overruns'. The impact of waterlogging and salinity on irrigated land, the report said, can be 'severe, long-term and often permanent'.[6]

The World Bank's lending to forest projects is also controversial. In response to the rapid rate of deforestation, and criticisms that its lending was causing some of that deforestation, the Bank launched the Tropical Forestry Action Plan in 1985, in conjunction with the FAO, the UN Development Programme and the World Resources Institute (a Washington-based NGO). The idea was to raise US$8 billion for forestry projects and to help countries to draw up their own national forestry plan. But the plan was drawn up with little input from environmental NGOs in countries affected by deforestation and 'seemed to embody every error of the top-down, socially oblivious and resource-destructive approach ... A survey in 1990 of nine national plans found that none of them would actually reduce deforestation'.[7]

The World Bank's record is, therefore, poor and it was hardly surprising that in 1995 a network of worldwide NGOs launched a campaign: 'fifty years is enough'. Some pressed for the Bank and IMF to be closed down in 1995, their 50th anniversary year. Others took the view that the organisations were capable of reform. At least 500 NGOs from South and North joined the campaign. All shared a common view, expressed by Juliette Majot of BankCheck, 'that the Bank as an institution should be a less powerful determinant of development'.[8]

The Bank survived but calls for its reform have increased, both in the corridors of official power, among NGOs and on the streets. In early 2000 a highly critical report of the IMF and the World Bank was published by the US Congressional International Financial Institution Advisory Commission. The majority of the eleven-member commission, including the commission's chairman Allan Meltzer and the distinguished economist Jeffrey Sachs of Harvard, called for vast downsizing of the operations of both institutions.

On the streets, huge protests at the Bank's spring meeting in 2000 were followed by protests in Prague in September that year at its annual meeting that hindered the movement of delegates and caused the meeting to be brought to a premature end. Protesters then forced the cancellation of a meeting the Bank planned to hold in Barcelona in June 2001. While Bank's staff were making many noises about how the institution was reforming its policies, there was still little evidence of this on the ground. The Bank needs to be downsized to remove the influence it has over economic sectors that are vital to the poor.

UNITED NATIONS AGENCIES

Food and Agriculture Organisation (FAO)

The Rome-based Food and Agriculture Organization is the largest specialised agency in the United Nations system. With a mandate to raise levels of nutrition and standards of living, to improve agricultural productivity, and to better the condition of rural populations, it is the lead UN agency for agriculture, forestry, fisheries and rural development.

The FAO gives technical assistance to help increase food production. It says that its specific priority is to encourage sustainable agriculture and rural development, increase food production and food security, while conserving and managing natural resources. 'The aim is to meet the needs of both present and future generations by promoting development that does not degrade the environment and is technically appropriate, economically viable and socially acceptable'.[9] It set up a Special Programme for Food Security in 1994 which is now operational in 62 member countries. The FAO organised the 1996 World Food Summit and the World Food Summit+5 meeting.

Employing around 6,000 people at its Rome headquarters and several thousand more in the field, the FAO has attracted the criticism that it is bureaucratic and that farmer organisations in developing countries have little input into its work.

International Fund for Agricultural Development (IFAD)

The UN's Rome-based International Fund for Agricultural Development was set up following a World Food Conference in 1974 and given a mandate of combating hunger and rural poverty in low-income food-deficit countries. It gives loans and makes grants to increase food production and improve the nutritional levels of the poorest peoples. IFAD was the first UN agency to be jointly funded by Western and oil-exporting countries, belonging to the Organisation of Petroleum Exporting Countries.

In total, IFAD has financed 578 projects in 115 countries, giving about US$7.2 billion in grants and loans, mostly on highly concessional terms, repayable over 40 years. Two-fifths of its loans have gone to Sub-Saharan Africa, a quarter to Asia and the Pacific, a fifth to Latin America and the Caribbean and just under a fifth to the Middle East and North Africa. IFAD has funded low-cost credit schemes and less fashionable agricultural research that tries to increase the yields of foods on which the poorest rely. It has also worked closely with NGOs.

'By responding to the expectations of its clients, the rural poor, and with their active participation, the Fund strives to design and implement innovative, cost-effective and reapplicable programmes that have a sustainable impact'.[10] But IFAD's rhetoric sometimes runs ahead of performance. Its loans have not always succeeded in reaching the poor; they are channelled through governments to local finance institutions which often favour the better-off rather than the very poorest.

World Food Programme (WFP)

The world's largest international food aid organisation, the Rome-based WFP describes itself as 'the frontline United Nations organisation fighting to eradicate world hunger'. The WFP says that its mission is to save the lives of people caught up in humanitarian crises, through Food-For-Life; to support the most vulnerable people at the most critical times of their lives, through Food-For-Growth; and to help the hungry poor become self-reliant and build assets, through Food-For-Work. In 2000, the programme helped to feed more than 83 million people in 83 countries. Food aid in the form of direct shipments of cereals totalled 9.5 million tonnes.

The WFP says that it uses food aid as 'a vital catalyst in development activities that promote self-reliance among the poorest of the poor who are often bypassed by more mainstream development'.[11] Most of its work, however, is now in distributing food to keep people alive in emergencies. Sub-Saharan Africa received most of the emergency food which went to conflict-affected countries during the 1990s. A decade ago, two out of three tonnes of the food aid provided by the WFP was used for helping people become self-reliant. Today, that picture is reversed; 80 per cent of WFP resources are used for victims of man-made disasters. While food aid can be vital in emergencies and conflict situations – as in Afghanistan in late 2001 – it makes only a small contribution to food security overall. And unless given to meet a specific need, food aid can damage the market for farmers in the recipient country.

CHAPTER 16

CONCLUSION:
AGRICULTURE MATTERS

Will the world continue to watch the hungry people of
the world die silently?

FAO Director-General, Jacques Diouf

WHY PRIORITISE AGRICULTURE?

Agriculture matters. It matters because it produces the food that
feeds people and provides most of the jobs and incomes on which
the world's most vulnerable people depend. Small-scale agriculture
matters above all because it is the base of survival for the poor and a
key part of overcoming poverty. It matters because the absence of a
viable agricultural sector makes it less attractive for people to stay in
the rural areas; it matters because it can stem the drift to towns and
cities. Agriculture matters because a depressed agricultural sector can
give rise to social instability, civic disorder, conflict, and war. Agriculture matters because the continuation of poverty is in no one's
interests.

Policymakers have a clear responsibility to agriculture. And yet as
important as it is, developing country agriculture is prone to neglect
by both governments and the international community. Over the last
three decades, many Third World governments have reduced their
spending on agriculture, while donors have reduced their aid to the
sector. But in 1974, governments at a major world food conference
in Rome resolved to take action to ensure that within a decade no

child would go to bed hungry and no family would fear for its next day's bread. 'History will judge the adequacy of our policies and actions in relation to this pledge', said the conference Secretary-general.

History is judging. And the numbers speak for themselves. Policies and actions have proved grossly inadequate. Much of the analysis in this book has pointed to a bleak outlook for developing country agriculture. Policymakers cannot escape their responsibility for this state of affairs. But some of the analysis also shows the huge potential, a potential that could overcome the negative aspects. Governments have a responsibility to encourage this. The world has the productive capacity to produce enough food for all, but governments have not allocated the resources that are needed. The political will has been missing.

The beginning of the twenty-first century is a time when the world is richer than ever, better connected than ever, in terms of communication, and more knowledgeable than ever. In this world of unprecedented wealth the degree of poverty and deprivation is a disgrace. Never before in history is there such a capacity to eradicate hunger and poverty. 'Hunger is one problem we can actually solve', points out David Beckman, president of Bread for the World; 'for the first time in history we have the resources and the technology to do it'.[1]

According to the FAO, the potential for achieving the 1996 World Food Summit goal of halving the number of hungry people by 2015 remains good, but it will require the eradication of hunger to be adopted 'as a specific objective nationally and internationally within poverty reduction strategies ... The lead must come from the families, communities and countries where food insecurity is deepest, but their efforts must be matched with reciprocal resource commitments by the international community, provided through bilateral and multi-lateral channels and civil society organisations ... getting rid of hunger is a precondition for success in poverty alleviation'.[2]

In many developing countries, especially in Sub-Saharan Africa, up to half the population lives below the poverty line. 'In these circumstances, sustained growth can be achieved only by creating conditions in which poor groups, largely poor farmers, herders and so on, can increase productivity and output'.[3] This is a message that governments should heed.

AID THAT WORKS

While governments of Western countries were among those who committed themselves to the World Food Summit target in 1996, they were also cutting the development aid that would help the target to be reached. In the 1990s aid to agriculture fell significantly as a proportion of overall development assistance, 'from about 20 per cent in the late 1980s to about 12 per cent today ... The declining support for agriculture is extremely damaging to efforts to reduce poverty and hunger'.[4]

The share of aid going to low-income or least developed countries, which are home to 85 per cent of the poor, 'stayed around 63 per cent (over the period 1988–98) and agricultural aid collapsed. The rural sector has largely remained neglected'.[5] Yet it would seem natural 'that to have a substantial effect on poverty, domestic investment and external assistance alike should focus on the rural areas where the poor live and on agriculture, the basis of their survival'.[6]

Instead of giving wholehearted support to small-scale agriculture, donors sometimes appear instead to be looking for some magic bullet to defeat poverty. In doing so they are in danger of turning their backs on the sector where most people earn a living and where the scope for improved productivity is considerable. But donors seem stubborn; 'it is extremely difficult to persuade donors to make the necessary commitments (to agriculture) in spite of the priority all claim to give to poverty alleviation', says FAO Director-general, Jacques Diouf.[7]

If the 1996 target is to be achieved, then more aid needs to go to resource-poor smallholder farmers. Dr Diouf has called on donors to contribute to a Trust Fund for Food Security with an initial amount of US$500 million to support agriculture in developing countries. He believes this amount is necessary to accelerate the process to-wards the 2015 goal. But it still falls a long way short of the US$3 billion a year in increased spending that the FAO estimated in 1996 was necessary to meet the target.

More assistance should go especially to help replicate successful small-scale farmer initiatives. This is vital in the task of growing more food to benefit the people who most need it. Donor aid money should be reoriented so that a much higher proportion is used for this purpose. The World Bank's sizable funds (see Chapter 15) could bring enormous benefits if they were targeted at replicating initiatives that help small-farmer agriculture. In view of the Bank's poor record in helping this sector, donors should switch funds from the Bank to donors, including NGOs, who can make a difference.

Aid policies need to be much more sensitive and targeted to help the poor. Large agencies, such as the World Bank, should reconsider policies such as structural adjustment programmes and debt repayment enforcement that cut across and undermine their policies on food, agriculture, rural development and poverty elimination.

An Economic Environment that Does Not Hinder

While more assistance is needed from both donors and governments of developing countries, changes have to run deeper. Given that agriculture matters, it follows that the factors which affect agriculture also matter a great deal. The economic environment must help, not hinder, and changes are needed in this wider environment.

Many developing countries are having to use scarce resources in order to repay foreign debts rather than use those resources for pressing needs such as food-crop agriculture. While some governments of developing countries treat agriculture as a poor relation, despite its vital importance, others would devote more funds to the sector if these were available.

The recent history of debt relief makes for depressing reading. Under the World Bank/IMF Heavily Indebted Poor Countries (HIPC) initiative, 22 out of 52 indebted countries have received debt relief packages. This relieves some – by no means all – of their debt, and the HIPC initiative recognises only 41 countries, rather than 52, as indebted. Even the 22 selected countries will have to wait for several years, until they have poverty reduction strategies that satisfy World Bank and IMF criteria, before their debt is finally written off. The 52 countries have debts of US$375 billion; it costs them about $24 billion a year to service those debts — to repay interest and capital on them. Most is owed to government departments in Western countries, to the World Bank, IMF and aid agencies.

In 1999 the Group of Seven industrialised nations promised at their summit in Cologne to cancel US$110 billion of debt. The 22 countries that have qualified for debt relief are relatively small, with a combined population of around 205 million. But the 52 most heavily indebted countries have a joint population of more than 1,030 million. Countries enjoying a reduction in annual debt servicing account, therefore, for only 20 per cent of the population of the 52 countries. The reduction, some $800 million, amounts to only 3.4 per cent of the total annual debt service payment of the 52. Among the 19 countries on the HIPC list that have yet to qualify are war-torn states such as Burundi, Ethiopia, Sudan and Vietnam.

The HIPC initiative 'is not deep enough to provide a lasting exit to the debt burdens faced by indebted countries. It moves far too slowly and is subject to increasingly discredited IMF austerity conditions'.[8] Sixteen of the 22 countries with debt packages will still be spending more each year on debt repayment than on healthcare. Eleven countries lie outside the HIPC initiative, including Bangladesh, Haiti and Nigeria, whose debt profiles are not considered serious enough, yet who are in urgent need of debt cancellation. Nigeria's debt per head is about US$250, higher than at least six HIPC qualifiers and more than twice that of Burkina Faso, a qualifying country.

This slow pace of debt relief, and the continuing flow of funds from the poor to rich countries 'is immoral and profoundly unjust', says Camille Chalmers of Haiti's Jubilee 2000 campaign for debt relief.[9] Substantial progress is needed if the poor are to be freed from the debt shackles which were none of their making. The 1996 World Food Summit target cannot be met 'unless rich nations increase aid and lift crippling debt burdens', says Harsh Mander, director of Action Aid's programme in India.[10]

Substantial changes are needed in the World Trade Organisation and in policies on transnational corporations. The WTO, as it was created, is a 'one horse' organisation, concerned only with trade liberalisation. But the horse is trampling on the poor. The WTO is impotent to protect developing countries from the fall in prices of primary agricultural produce, on which many depend for the bulk of their foreign earnings. It is also based on the assumption that it is countries who trade, not companies (see Chapter 12). The WTO has no role in regulating the activities of TNCs, which often get their way in an organisation where developing countries are poor relations.

The WTO's 1995 Trade-Related Intellectual Property Rights (TRIPs) agreement, for example, was strongly opposed by developing countries. TRIPs grants patent holders the right to protect their intellectual property in WTO member states. This includes the crops which TNCs have patented in increasing numbers. It was the corporations that wanted the agreement and which were powerful enough to get it – and to set the rules of an organisation that is powerless to regulate them. WTO rules need to ban patents on crops.

In his book, 'Fast Food Nation', Eric Schlosser says that whereas the twentieth century was dominated by a struggle against totalitarian systems of state power, so the twenty-first will be marked 'by a struggle to curtail excessive corporate power'. The poor at least deserve an international trade organisation that is part of that struggle.[11]

In theory the WTO is a 'one-member country, one-vote democracy'; in practice there has never been a vote in its six years' existence. Developing country members could vote to change the rules to make the WTO a trade organisation that is capable of grappling with the most pressing trade issues affecting the world's poor. Or it might be better to scrap the WTO and start afresh.

A NEW DIRECTION

The encouragement of smallholder agriculture needs to be seen as a central part of poverty-reduction strategies. In the 1996 World Food Summit declaration, governments warned that hunger and food

insecurity 'are likely to persist, and even increase dramatically …
unless urgent, determined and concerted action is taken'. Governments have not taken such action and the 1996 target is in jeopardy.
They need to heed their own warning. Against a background of an
unfavourable economic and physical environment, the target will be
rescued only by much greater priority at both national and international levels, and by genuine attention to the wider issues that
affect food security. If people go hungry today, it is at least partly
because governments have decided to spend money on and give
greater priority to other things.

'Statistics do not bleed', the novelist Arthur Koestler once said.
Numbers do not capture the 'bloody' suffering of every one of the
800 million undernourished and chronically hungry people. Progress
is too slow and in some ways the situation is worse than it was in
1996 at the time of the World Food Summit. Talk of halving the
number of hungry people in the world by 2015 is a pipe-dream
unless governments and the international community recognise the
urgency of the situation.

'The key issue is the direction of agriculture', says Kevin Blundell
of Christian Aid. 'We need the kind of agriculture that will allow the
possibility of meeting the target. We need changes in international
trade rules that allow developing countries to prioritise food security
over trade'.[12] It is time for policymakers to give agriculture a new
impetus, a new direction, to take it along a road where it can feed
the world's hungry. It can be done, the world knows how to do it.
Not to do so would be the ultimate betrayal of the poorest people
on earth.

Notes

Chapter 1

1. I am indebted to Jan Valkoun of the International Centre for Agricultural Research in the Dry Areas in Syria for this insight. There is some evidence that agriculture may have started even earlier.
2. World Bank website: http://www.worldbank.org
3. 'New economy, new agriculture', *Spore*, June 2000, Wageningen, The Netherlands: Technical Centre for Agricultural and Rural Cooperation (CTA).
4. *Rural Poverty Report 2001: the Challenge of Ending Rural Poverty*, Rome: IFAD, 2001.
5. Quoted in 'New economy, new agriculture', op. cit.
6. About half of the 12 million children under five who die each year are stunted by undernourishment, says the FAO's *The State of Food and Agriculture, 2000* (p. 199), that is, just over 16,400 a day.

Chapter 2

1. University of Illinois College website, 2000: http://www.aces.uiuc.edu/~sare/
2. C. Reijntjes, B. Haverkort and A. Waters-Bayer, *Farming for the Future*, London: Macmillan, 1992, p. 6.
3. D. Paarlberg, *Towards a Well-Fed World*, Iowa State University, 1988, p. 3.
4. C. Reijntjes, B. Haverkort and A. Waters-Bayer, op. cit.
5. E. Goldsmith, 'Development as colonialism', *The Ecologist*, March/April 1997, p. 69.
6. See M. A. Altieri, *Agroecology: the Science of Sustainable Agriculture*, London: Westview/IT Publications, 1995, p. 3.
7. C. Reijntjes, B. Haverkort and A. Waters-Bayer, op. cit., p. 7.
8. Ibid., p. 39.
9. *Agricultural Policies in OECD Countries: Monitoring and Evaluation 2001*, Paris: OECD, 2001.

10. John Vidal, 'Global trade focuses on exodus from the land', *Guardian*, 28 February 2001.

11. See Renée Vallvé, 'The decline of diversity in European agriculture', *The Ecologist*, March/April 1993.

12. M. A. Altieri, op. cit., p. 367. Jules Pretty, 'The real costs of modern farming', *Resurgence*, March/April 2001, puts the total cost of modern agriculture to the UK at £2.34 billion in 1996.

13. 'BSE persuades EU on eco-farming', *Financial Times*, 19 January 2001.

14. 'Shroeder urges shift in farm policy', *Financial Times*, 30 November 2000.

15. Nicholas George, 'Ethical practice may have kept Sweden clear', *Financial Times*, 30 November 2000.

16. See *The Organic Food and Farming Report, 2000*, Bristol: Soil Association, 2001.

17. *Eat This: Fresh Ideas on the WTO Agreement on Agriculture*, RSPB, March 2001.

18. Marilyn Carr, *The AT Reader*, London: Intermediate Technology Publications, 1985, p. 148.

19. See 'Farm methods hurt future food output', *Financial Times*, 15 February 2001.

20. Howard Shapiro, 'Voice in the wilderness', *Waitrose Food Illustrated*, November 2000.

CHAPTER 3

1. FAO estimates, 2000.

2. *Rural Poverty Report 2001: the Challenge of Ending Rural Poverty*, Rome: IFAD, 2001, p. 22.

3. 'The wonders of wheat', *World Bank News*, 9 November 1995, Paris: The World Bank.

4. Communication to author, June 2001.

5. See John Madeley, *Hungry for Trade*, London: Zed Books, 2001, pp. 53–5.

6. Simon Maxwell and Adrian Fernando, 'Researching the controversial', *International Agricultural Development*, January/February 1990.

7. *Trade and Hunger: an Overview of Case Studies*, Forum Syd, Stockholm 2000.

8. Chris Evans, *Grihasthashram Newsletter*, Nepal: Jajarkot Permaculture Programme, December 1999.

9. M. A. Altieri, *Agroecology: the Science of Sustainable Agriculture*, London: Westview/IT Publications, 1995, p. 107.

10. Ibid.

11. Speech to Women in Agriculture conference, Washington, June/July 1998.

12. Hans Carlier, *Understanding Traditional Agriculture*, Leusden: ILEIA, 1987,

p. 10.

13. See J. Bunders, B. Haverkort and W. Hiemstra (eds), *Biotechnology; Building on Farmers' Knowledge*, London: Macmillan/ILEIA, 1996.

14. Fiona Hinchcliffe, John Thompson and Jules N. Pretty, *Sustainable Agriculture and Food Security in East and Southern Africa*, London: International Institute for Environment and Development, 1986.

15. Jules Pretty, *Regenerating Agriculture*, London: Earthscan, 1995, p. 3.

16. Interview with author, January 2001.

17. Fiona Hinchcliffe, John Thompson and Jules N. Pretty, 'Sustainability: the way ahead', *International Agricultural Development*, September/October 1996.

18. See *International Agricultural Development*, July/August 1996; also Vandana Shiva, 'Globalization and poverty', *Resurgence*, September/October 2000.

19. See Seeds of Change website: http://www.seedsofchange.com

20. David Cooper, Renée Vallvé and Henk Hobbelink (eds), *Growing Diversity*, London: IT Publications/GRAIN, 1992, p. 5.

21. *People, Plants and Patents*, Report of the Crucible Group, IDRC, Canada, 1994, p. 24.

22. *Global Biodiversity Assessment*, UNDP, Cambridge University Press, 1995.

23. Fiona Hinchcliffe, John Thompson and Jules N. Pretty, op. cit.

24. David Cooper, Renée Vallvé and Henk Hobbelink (eds), op. cit., p. 7.

CHAPTER 4

1. Caroline Maria de Jesus, *Child of the Dark*, the diary of a Brazilian slum dweller.

2. *The State of Food Insecurity in the World*, Rome: FAO, 2000.

3. Ibid.

4. Ibid.

5. *The State of Food and Agriculture, 2000*, Rome: FAO, 2000, p. 308.

6. Speech to World Agricultural Forum, St Louis, May 2001.

7. Paper prepared for an Inter-Parliamentary Conference, Rome: FAO, 29 November–2 December, 1998.

8. *The State of Food Insecurity in the World*, op. cit.

9. Ibid.

10. Africa Watch, *Africa Recovery*, New York: United Nations, 1998.

11. *The State of Food and Agriculture, 2000*, op. cit., p. 3.

12. Speech to Overseas Development Institute, London, May 2001.

13. Ibid.

14. Press Release, PR 01/34e, Rome, FAO, 24 May 2001.

15. M.S. Swiminathan, *One Planet*, BBC World Service, 5 January 2000.

16. *The State of Food and Agriculture, 2000*, op.cit., pp 308–12.

17. Jules Pretty and Rachael Hine, *Feeding the World with Sustainable Agriculture: a Summary of New Evidence*, University of Essex, October 2000.

CHAPTER 5

1. M. A. Altieri, M. A. Altieri, *Agroecology: the Science of Sustainable Agriculture*, London: Westview/IT Publications, 1995.
2. Jules Pretty and Rachael Hine, *Feeding the World with Sustainable Agriculture: a Summary of New Evidence*, University of Essex, October 2000.
3. University of Essex, Safe-World Research Project ('The Potential for Sustainable Agriculture to Feed the World'), Case Studies, Essex, October 2000.
4. Conversation with author, October 1991.
5. A directory of world-wide permaculture institutions can be obtained from Permaculture International Ltd, PO Box 6039, South Lismore, NSW 2480, Australia; fax: 0061 66 220579; email: pcjournal@peg.apc.org.
6. Conversation with author, February 1991.
7. From paper by Sebastién Rafaralahy, presented to conference on Reducing Poverty through Sustainable Agriculture, London, January 2001.
8. Food for Hungry International, quoted in the Safe-World Research Project Case Studies, op. cit.
9. Laura S Meitzner and Martin L. Price, *Amaranth to Zai Holes; Ideas for Growing Food Under Difficult Conditions*, North Fort Myers, USA: ECHO, 1996.
10. 'Deep dig in Nepal: yields rise four-fold', *International Agricultural Development*, May/June 1998.
11. 'Rediscovering organic farming in India', *International Agricultural Development*, May/June 1998.
12. Chris Evans, 'When success becomes apparent', *International Agricultural Development*, March/April 1997.
13. Website: http://www.msnepal.org/partners/jpp
14. *The State of Food Insecurity in the World*, Rome: FAO, 2000.
15. Miguel Altieri, 'Applying agroecology to enhance the productivity of peasant farming systems in Latin America', paper presented to conference on Reducing Poverty though Sustainable Agriculture, London, January 2001.
16. From Maria Victoria Arboleda, 'Rainforest solutions', *Permaculture Magazine*, No. 13, 1996.

CHAPTER 6

1. Cornelis van Tuyll, 'Agricultural research has no lobby', *Agriculture+Rural Development*, 1/2001, Frankfurt.
2. Robert Chambers and Jules Pretty, 'Will the opportunity be seized?', *International Agricultural Development*, November/December 1994, p. 9. See also Institute of Development Studies (IDS) Discussion Paper, 334, *Towards a Learning Paradigm: New Professionalism and Institutions for Agriculture*, 1993.

3. CGIAR News, Washington, October 1999.
4. CGIAR News, Washington, December 1999.
5. IRRI Hotline, Vol. 10, No. 3, September 2000, Manila: IRRI.
6. 'Filipinos call for the closure of IRRI', *Utusan Konsumer*, Penang, August 2000.
7. 'IRRI documents showed grants received from chemical companies', *Utusan Konsumer*, February 2001.
8. See for example, 'Lowland could give high yields', *International Agricultural Development*, May/June 1994.
9. See John Madeley, *Hungry for Trade*, London: Zed Books, 2001, pp. 148–9.
10. See Z. Khalikulov *et al.*, 'Naturing the Vavilov legacy', *Caravan*, December 2000, Syria: ICARDA.
11. Robert Chambers and Jules Petty, op. cit.
12. Jillian Lenné and David Wood, *International Agricultural Development*, March/April 1995.
13. Conversation with author, March 2001.
14. Mae-Wan Ho, *Genetic Engineering: Dream or Nightmare*, Penang: Third World Network, 1998, p. 45.
15. CGIAR News, Washington, October 2000.
16. Conversation with author, March 2001.
17. *Robbing Coffee's Cradle – GM Coffee and its Threat to Poor Farmers*, London: Action Aid, May 2001.
18. Ibid.
19. Communication with author, May 2001.
20. IRRI Press Release, January 2001.
21. Paul Brown, 'GM rice promoters have gone too far', *The Guardian*, 10 February 2001.
22. *Grains of Delusion: Golden Rice Seen from the Ground*, GRAIN and other agencies, 2001; website: www.grain.org/publications/reports/delusion, htm
23. Ibid.
24. Andrew Simms, *Selling Suicide*, London: Christian Aid, 1999.
25. Rural Advancement Foundation International (Canada) website, 2001: http://www.rafi.org
26. *Communiqué*, June 1999.
27. Quoted by George Monbiot in 'Biotech has bamboozled us all', *The Guardian*, 24 August 2000.

CHAPTER 7

1. FAO website, 2001: http://www.fao.org
2. 'More crops with less water', *Spore*, August 1977, Wageningen: CTA.
3. Speech to the Chief Ministers of India 1986; quoted in *Report of the Independent Review: Sardar Sarovar*, Resource Futures International Inc., Canada, 1992.

4. *Dams and Development*, World Commission on Dams, Cape Town, WCD, November 2000.

5. Ibid.

6. Ibid.

7. 'After WCD launch: critics demand dam-building moratorium', NGO statement, November 2000.

8. Conversation with author, November 2000.

9. Intermediate Technology Development Group, website, 2001: http://www.oneworld.org/itdg

10. See John Madeley, 'Farmers use the force of flow', *Financial Times*, 1 April 1998.

11. *Treadle Pumps for Irrigation in Africa*, January 2001, Rome, FAO: http://www.fao.org/iptrid/treadle/treadle pumps.pdf

12. 'More crops with less water', op. cit.

13. FAKT Focus Newsletter 15, Association for Appropriate Technologies, Germany, 1996.

14. See 'More yield and profit from run-off harvesting', *International Agricultural Development*, November/December 1991.

15. Laura S Meitzner and Martin L. Price, *Amaranth to Zai Holes; Ideas for Growing Food Under Difficult Conditions*, North Fort Myers, USA: ECHO, 1996, p. 187.

16. See John Madeley, 'Drink in the atmosphere', *Financial Times*, 1 May 2000. The Meteorological Service of Canada produces a Fog newsletter, website: www.mscsmc.ec.gc.calarmp/

17. Shahridan Faiez, 'Indigenous water knowledge drains away', *International Agricultural Development*, January/February 1996.

18. John Thompson, 'A handful of water cannot be grasped', *International Agricultural Development*, November/December 1991.

19. John Madeley, 'Will rice turn the Sahel to salt?', *New Scientist*, 9 October 1993.

20. FAO website, op. cit.

21. Conversation with author, May 2001.

22. Dr Chris Scott, IWMI researcher leading this project. IMWI website: http://www.iwmi.org

23. 'Water: a scarce resource', *International Agricultural Development*, January/February 1996.

24. 'South Asia: reforms urgently needed', *International Agricultural Development*, January/February 1996.

25. *Rural Poverty Report 2001: the Challenge of Ending Rural Poverty*, Rome: IFAD, 2001, p. 98.

CHAPTER 8

1. *Rural Poverty Report 2001: the Challenge of Ending Rural Poverty*, Rome: IFAD, 2001, p. 79.

2. N. Dudley, J. Madeley and S. Stolton, *Land is Life: Land Reform and Sustainable Agriculture*, Intermediate Technology Publications, 1992.

3. Frances Moore Lappé and Joseph Collins, *Food First*, London: Abacus, 1982.

4. Liz Alden Wily, *Land Tenure Reform and the Balance of Power in Eastern and Southern Africa*, Overseas Development Institute: Natural Resource Perspectives, Number 58, London: ODI, June 2000.

5. *Rural Poverty Report 2001*, op. cit.

6. Website: http://ns.sdnhon.org.hn/miembros/via/cartas-en.htm

7. N. Dudley, J. Madeley and S. Stolton, op. cit., p. 145.

8. Statement presented to the International Conference on Agrarian Reform and Rural Development, Philippines, December 2000.

9. Food First 'Backgrounder', Institute for Food and Development Policy, Oakland, California, June 2000; website: http://www.foodfirst.org/pubs/backgrdrs/2001/w01v7n1.html

10. Jochen Donner, 'Access to land – innovative land reforms as a contribution to reducing poverty', *Agriculture+Rural Development*, 2/2000, Frankfurt.

11. Vilmar Schneider: http://www.fian.org

12. Lino de David, 'Agrarian reform in Brazil', in *Land is Life*, pp. 59–69.

13. See *Trade and Hunger*, Stockholm: Forum Syd, 2000; *The Impact of Trade Liberalisation on Food Security in the South*, Brussels: CIDSE, May 2001, and John Madeley, *Hungry for Trade*, London: Zed Books, pp. 73–90.

14. Boua Chanthou, 'Impacts of trade liberalisation on Malaysia, Philippines and Cambodia', in *Trade and Hunger*, op. cit.

15. Popular Coalition to Eradicate Hunger and Poverty, *The Land Poor*, Rome: IFAD, 2000, p. 4.

CHAPTER 9

1. 'Women's advances in agriculture', *Spore*, August 1998, Wageningen: CTA.

2. *The State of Food Insecurity in the World*, Rome: FAO, 2000.

3. Senait Seyoum, 'Gender issues in food security in Ethiopia', *Reflections*, No. 4, December 2000, Addis Ababa/Nairobi: Panos Ethiopia/Heinrich Boll Foundation, p. 40.

4. FAO website.

5. *Rural Poverty Report 2001: the Challenge of Ending Rural Poverty*, Rome: IFAD, 2001, p. 28

6. *Gender Perspectives: Focus on the Rural Poor*, Rome: IFAD, May 2000, p. 3.

7. 'Women's advances in agriculture', op. cit.

8. FAO Plan of Action for Women in Development, 1996–2001, Rome: FAO, 1995.

9. *Gender Perspectives*, op. cit. p. 7.

10. *Rural Poverty Report 2001*, op. cit., p. 30.

11. Ibid., p. 29.
12. Ibid., p. 30.
13. Ibid., p. 29.
14. Marilyn Carr (ed.), *Women and Food Security: the Experience of SADCC Countries*, London: IT Publications, 1991, p. 17.
15. Conversation with author, July 1988.
16. 'Women's work – feeding the world', Washington: Future Harvest; website: http://www.futureharvest.org
17. 'A women's place', *International Agricultural Development*, January/February 1993.

CHAPTER 10

1. *Rural Poverty Report 2001: the Challenge of Ending Rural Poverty*, Rome: IFAD, 2001, p. 208.
2. *The Future for Microfinance*, Panos Media Briefing, No. 21, London: The Panos Institute, 1997.
3. Chief Bisi Ogunleye, 'Creating wealth through credit', *International Agricultural Development*, March/April 1996.
4. Conversation with author, October 1998.
5. Conversations with author, September 1998.
6. Kieran Cooke, 'Fluctuating fortunes', *Financial Times*, 8 December 1994.
7. Based on conversations with Zambian farmers, 1996.

CHAPTER 11

1. *Rural Poverty Report 2001: the Challenge of Ending Rural Poverty*, Rome: IFAD, 2001, p. 102.
2. *Agenda for Change*, Geneva: Centre for our Common Future, 1992, p. 25.
3. *HIV/AIDS and Agriculture: an FAO Perspective – The Socio-Economic Impact of HIV/AIDS on Agriculture*. Rome: FAO, 2000; http://www.fao.org/docrep/meeting/003/Y0310E.htm
4. Ibid.
5. African Medical and Research Foundation, *Annual Review*, 2000. London: AMREF.
6. Solar Photovoltaics for Sustainable Agriculture and Rural Development, FAO, 2000.
7. FAO website: http://www.fao.org
8. Stephen Mandel, 'Not by roads alone', *International Agricultural Development*, January/February 1989.

CHAPTER 12

1. Angus Maddison, *Monitoring the World Economy*, Paris: OECD, 1995.
2. Susan George, *The Lugano Report*, London: Pluto Press, 1999, p. 105.
3. 'India desperate to export rice', *Financial Times*, 21 December 2000.

4. *Food and International Trade*, Rome: FAO, 1996.
5. WTO website: http://www.wto.org
6. Communication to author.
7. Hezron Nyangito, 'Impact of Uruguay (Round) Agreement on Agriculture on Food Security: the case of Kenya', in *Trade and Hunger – An Overview of Case Studies on the Impact of Trade Liberalisation on Food Security*, Stockholm: Forum Syd, 2000; http://www.forumsyd.se/globala.htm See also *The Impact of Trade Liberalisation on Food Security in the South*, Brussels: CIDSE, May 2001.
8. See John Madeley, *Hungry for Trade*, London: Zed Books, Chapter 5, for further and more detailed examples.
9. *Courier*, special issue, *Food for Development*, 'The Right to Protection', January–February 1998, Brussels: European Commission.
10. Sophia Murphy *et al.*, *Food Security and Trade Liberalisation: an Agenda for Multilateral Trade Rules*, Brussels: CIDSE, June 2001.
11. From *The Ecologist*, May/June 2000.
12. See Cargill's website.
13. Calculated from World Bank figures in *World Development Report, 2000/2001*, Washington: World Bank, 2000.
14. B. Kneen, *Invisible Giant*, London: Pluto Press, 1996.
15. B. Kneen, chapter in *Hungry for Power*, London: UK Food Group, 1999.
16. Ibid.
17. 'Crops and Robbers, biopiracy and the patenting of staple food crops', London: Action Aid, November 1999.
18. *Globalisation and Liberalisation*, Geneva: UNCTAD, 1996.
19. Figure from the FairTrade Foundation, London
20. 'Export taxes on primary products', Commonwealth paper no 9. London: Commonwealth Secretariat, 1984.

CHAPTER 13

1. *The Challenge of Climate Change: Poor Farmers at Risk*, IPCC, May 2001.
2. Speech to Consultative Group on International Agricultural Research (CGIAR) conference, Durban, May 2001.
3. 'Africa Watch', *Africa Recovery*, New York: United Nations, 1998.
4. John Madeley, 'Jordan presses the importance of olives', *Financial Times*, 29 June 2001.
5. Ibid.
6. Interview with David Peppiat, British Red Cross, April 2000.
7. For a description of soil, see John Bede Harrison, *Growing Food Organically*, Vancouver: Waterwheel Press, 1993.
8. FAO website: http://www.fao.org
9. Tom Wakeford, Green Futures, January/February 2001.
10. International Institute of Tropical Agriculture website, http://www.cgiar.org.iita

11. Hosny El-Lakany, Assistant Director-general (Forestry Department), FAO Press Release, PR 01/38, June 2001.

12. John Madeley, *Hungry for Trade*, London: Zed Books, p. 31.

13. The Crucible Group, *Peoples, Plants and Patents*, Canada: International Development Research Centre, 1994.

14. Farmers World Network, *What Variety!*, April 1996.

15. FAO Press Release, 00/45, Global Forest Resources Assessment 2000, Rome: FAO, August 2000.

16. Stephen Vosti, 'The role of agriculture in saving the rainforest', IFPRI, 2020 Brief 9, 1995, Washington: IFPRI, 1995.

17. Nigel Sizer and Jose Goldemberg, 'Squander mongers', *The Guardian*, 25 March 1998.

CHAPTER 14

1. *Rural Poverty Report 2001: the Challenge of Ending Rural Poverty*, Rome: IFAD, 2001, p. 99.

2. R. Trevor Wilson, Livestock Production Systems, London: CTA/Macmillan, 1995, p. 1.

3. *Livestock and Sustainable Agriculture*, FAO fact sheet, Rome: FAO, 1995.

4. John Bishop, 'Chickens: backyard production in the humid tropics' in Laura S. Meitzner and Martin L. Price, *Amaranth to Zai Holes*, p. 242.

5. Quoted in 'How bees help agriculture', *International Agricultural Development*, July/August 1989.

6. Paul Starkey, 'Networking for animal traction', *International Agricultural Development*, January/February 1993.

7. P. Starkey, E. Mwenya, J. Stares (eds), *Improving Animal Traction Technology*, Wageningen: CTA, 1994, p. 24.

8. FAO website: http://www.fao.org

9. World Watch List for Domestic Animal Diversity, 3rd edition, Rome: FAO, 2001.

10. Lester R Brown, 'The Future of Growth', *State of the World 1998*, Washington: Worldwatch Institute, p. 12.

11. Ibid.

12. *China's Food Economy to the Twenty-First Century: Supply, Demand and Trade*, Washington: IFPRI, 1997. Other studies have come to broadly similar conclusions; see, for example, Vaclav Smil, *Feeding the World: a Challenge for the Twenty-First Century*, Cambridge MA: MIT Press, 2000.

13. Lester R. Brown, *Tough Choices*, London: Earthscan, 1996, p. 133.

14. For a detailed description of the connections between the intensive farming of animals and world food supply, see G. Tansey and J. D'Silva (eds), *The Meat Business*, London: Earthscan, 1999.

15. Figures from the FAO; see, e.g. Press Release 01/54e, 21 September 2001.

16. *The State of Food and Agriculture, 2000*, p. 28.

17. Beatrice Gorez, 'Fisheries: the incoherencies', *Brussels Blind Spot*, Brussels: Aprodev, 1999.
18. Quoted in *Fish: A Net Loss for the Poor*, Panos Institute briefing paper, London, 1995.
19. Commodity Market Review, 1998–9, Rome: FAO, 1999.
20. Communication to author, 1999.
21. Interview with author, 1998.
22. *Fish: A Net Loss for the Poor*, op. cit.

CHAPTER 15

1. *Annual Report 2000*, Washington: World Bank, 2000.
2. *The Economist*, 12 October 1991.
3. World Bank News Release, 16 November 2000.
4. Alex Wilks, speech to Development-induced Displacement and Impoverishment conference, Oxford, January 1995.
5. See, for example, *World Rivers Review*, Vol. 12, No. 3, June 1997, Berkeley: World Rivers Network.
6. *Dams and Development*.
7. Bruce Rich, *Mortgaging the Earth*, London: Earthscan, 1994, p. 163.
8. A newsletter with NGO views on the Bank and Fund. See also J. Madeley, D. Sullivan and J. Woodruffe, *Who Runs the World?*, London: Christian Aid, 1995.
9. FAO website: http://www.fao.org
10. *Annual Report 2000*, Rome: IFAD, 2001.
11. WFP website: http://www.wfp.org

CHAPTER 16

1. *Foreign Aid to End Hunger*, Washington: Bread for the World, 2001.
2. *Fostering the Political Will to Fight Hunger*, Rome: FAO, May 2001.
3. Fawzi H. Al-Sultan, Foreword to *Rural Poverty Report 2001*, p. v.
4. Ibid., p. iv.
5. *Rural Poverty Report 2001*, p. 1.
6. Fawzi H Al-Sultan, op. cit, p. iv.
7. Jacques Diouf, *Go Between* newsletter, October–December 2000. Geneva: UN Non-Governmental Liaison Service.
8. John Madeley, 'No end to shackles', *The Observer*, 21 January 2001.
9. Ibid.
10. Communication to author, July 2001.
11. Eric Schlosser, *Fast Food Nation*, London: Allen Lane, 2001, p. 261.
12. Conversation with author, July 2001.

FURTHER READING

Altieri, M.A., *Agroecology: the Science of Sustainable Agriculture*, London: Westview/IT Publications, 1995.

Brown, Lester R., *Tough Choices*, London: Earthscan, 1996.

Bunders, J., B. Haverkort and W. Hiemstra (eds), *Biotechnology; Building on Farmers' Knowledge*, London: Macmillan/ILEIA, 1996.

Carlier, Hans, *Understanding Traditional Agriculture*, Leusden, Netherlands: ILEIA, 1987.

Carr, Marilyn (ed.), Women *and Food Security: the Experience of SADCC Countries*, London: IT Publications, 1991.

Cooper, David, Renée Vallvé and Henk Hobbelink (eds) *Growing Diversity*, London: IT Publications/GRAIN, 1992.

Devereux, S. and S. Maxwell, *Food Security in Sub-Saharan Africa*, London: ITDG Publishing/IDS, 2001.

Dudley, N., J. Madeley and S. Stolton, *Land is Life: Land Reform and Sustainable Agriculture*, London: IT Publications, 1992.

Harrison, John Bede, *Growing Food Organically*, Vancouver: Waterwheel Press, 1993.

Ho, Mae-Wan, *Genetic Engineering: Dream or Nightmare*, Penang: Third World Network, 1998.

Kneen, Brewster, *Invisible Giant*, London: Pluto Press, 1996.

Kotschi, J., A. Waters-Bayer, R. Adelhelm and U. Hoesle, *Ecofarming in Agricultural Development*, Eschborn: Verlag Josef Margraf, 1989.

Madeley, John, *Hungry for Trade*, London: Zed Books, 2001.

Meitzner, Laura S. and Martin L. Price, *Amaranth to Zai Holes; Ideas for Growing Food Under Difficult Conditions*, North Fort Myers: ECHO, 1996.

Pretty, Jules, *Regenerating Agriculture*, London: Earthscan, 1995.

Reij, C., I. Scoones and C. Toulmin, *Sustaining the Soil*, London: Earthscan, 1996.

Reijntjes, C., B. Haverkort and A. Waters-Bayer, *Farming for the Future*. London: Macmillan, 1992.
Schlosser, Eric, *Fast Food Nation: What the All-American Meal is Doing to the World*, London: Penguin, 2001.
Tansey, G. and J. D'Silva (eds), *The Meat Business*, London: Earthscan, 1999.
Whiteside, M., Living Farms: *Encouraging Sustainable Smallholders in Southern Africa*, London: Earthscan, 1999.

Reports

The Challenge of Climate Change: Poor Farmers at Risk, Geneva: Intergovernmental Panel on Climate Change, 2001.
Crops and Robbers, London: Action Aid, 2001.
Dams and Development, World Commission on Dams, Cape Town: WCD, November 2000.
Export Taxes on Primary Products, Commonwealth Paper No. 9. London: Commonwealth Secretariat, 1984.
Feeding the World with Sustainable Agriculture: A Summary of New Evidence, by Jules Pretty and Rachael Hine, University of Essex, October 2000.
Food Security and Trade Liberalisation: An Agenda for Multilateral Trade Rules, by Sophia Murphy et al., Brussels: CIDSE, 2001.
Foreign Aid to End Hunger, Washington: Bread for the World, 2001.
Fostering the Political Will to Fight Hunger, Rome: FAO, May 2001.
The Hidden Harvest: The Value of Wild Resources in Agricultural Systems, London: International Institute for Environment and Development, 1995.
HIV/AIDS and Agriculture: An FAO Perspective: The Socio-economic Impact of HIV/AIDS on Agriculture, Rome: FAO, 2000.
Human Development Report 2001, New York: UNDP.
The Impact of Trade Liberalisation on Food Security in the South, Brussels: CIDSE, 2001.
The Organic Food and Farming Report 2000, Bristol: Soil Association.
Robbing Coffee's Cradle – GM Coffee and its Threat to Poor Farmers, London: Action Aid, May 2001.
Rural Poverty Report 2001: The Challenge of Ending Rural Poverty, Rome: IFAD.
Selling Suicide, London: Christian Aid, 1999.
The State of Food and Agriculture, 2000, Rome: FAO, September 2000.
The State of Food Insecurity in the World 2000, Rome: FAO.
Sustainable Agriculture and Food Security in East and Southern Africa, by Fiona Hinchcliffe, John Thompson and Jules N. Pretty, London: International Institute for Environment and Development, 1986.
Trade and Hunger: An Overview of Case Studies, Stockholm: Forum Syd, 2000.
Treadle Pumps for Irrigation in Africa, Rome: FAO, January 2001.

Relevant Organisations Including Websites

Action Aid
  Hamlyn House, MacDonald Road, Archway, London N19 5PG:
  www.actionaid.org
Action Group on Erosion, Technology and Concentration
  (formerly Rural Advancement Foundation International) Canada:
  www.etcgroup.org

Bread for the World
  Box J, 1100 Wayne Avenue, Suite 1000, Silver Spring, MD 20910,
  USA: www.bread.org

Centre for Environment and Society
  University of Essex, Wivenhoe Park, Colchester CO4 3SQ UK:
  www.essex.ac.uk/centres/ces/

CGIAR (Consultative Group for International Agricultural Research)
  1818 H Street, NW, Washington DC, 20433, USA: www.cgiar.org

Christian Aid
  PO Box 100, London SE1 7RT: www.christian-aid.org.uk

CIDSE
  Rue Stevin, B-1000, Brussels, Belgium: www.cidse.org

Cornell International Institute for Agricultural Development
  Cornell University, Ithaca NY 14853, USA: www.cornell.edu

Fairtrade Foundation
  Suite 204, 16 Baldwin's Gardens, London ECIN 7RJ:
  www.fairtrade.org.uk

FAO
  Viale delle Terme di Caracalla, 00100, Rome, Italy: www.fao.org

FIAN
Foodfirst Information and Action Network: www.foodfirst.org

Focus on Global South
c/o CUSRI, Chulalongkorn University, Bangkok 10330, Thailand: www.focusweb.org

Friends of the Earth, 26-28 Underwood Street, London N1 7JQ: www.foe.co.uk

Future Harvest
www.futureharvest.org

GRAIN
Girona 25, pral., E-8010 Barcelona, Spain: www.grain.org

Greenpeace
Keizersgracht 176, 1016 DW Amsterdam, Netherlands: www.greenpeace.org

Institute for Agriculture and Trade Policy
2105 First Avenue South, Minneapolis, MN 55404-2505, USA: www.iatp.org/iatp

Intermediate Technology Development Group
Bourton, Rugby, CV23 9QZ, UK: www.oneworld.org/itdg

International Fund for Agricultural Development,
107 via del Serafino, 00142, Rome, Italy: www.ifad.org

Jajarkot Permaculture Project
Nepal. www.msnepal.org/partners/jpp

One World
website also includes organisations who are working on food issues: www.oneworld.org

Overseas Development Institute
111 Westminster Bridge Road, London SE1 7JD: www.odi.org.uk

Oxfam, GB
274 Banbury Road, Oxford, OX2 7DZ: www.oxfam.org.uk

Permaculture Association, UK
www.permaculture.org.uk

Permaculture International Ltd.
PO Box 6039 South Lismore, NSW 2480, Australia. Fax: 0061 66 220579. Email: pcjournal@peg.apc.org

Seeds of Change
www.seedsofchange.com

Third World Network
228 Macalister Street, 10400 Penang, Malaysia: www.twnside.org.sg

UK Food Group
  PO Box 100, London SE1 7RT: www.ukfg.org.uk

University of Illinois College
  www.aces.uiuc.edu/~sare/

Via Campesina
  E-mail: viacam@gbm.hn

World Bank
  1818 H Street NW, Washington DC, 20433 USA:
  www.worldbank.org

World Development Movement
  25 Beehive Place, London SW9 7QR: www.wdm.org.uk

World Food Programme
  www.wfp.org

World Trade Organisation
  Rue de Lausanne, Geneva, Switzerland: www.wto.org

INDEX

abattoirs, centralisation, 16
Abdouli, Abdelhamid, 132
Action Aid, 125, 164
Action for Development, Ethiopia, 39
Afghanistan, 34, 83, 159
Africa, 34; Congo Basin, 142;
    drought, 37; employment, 108;
    food production, 65; land tenure,
    87; maize, 22; mucuna cover crop,
    136; pearl millet, 23; Sahel region,
    23, 76, 138; soil degradation, 88;
    sub-Saharan, 33, 54, 67, 75, 91,
    116–17, 130, 158, 161; sub-Saharan
    species reduction, 146
African Traditional Responsive
    Banking, 103
agrarian reform, 85–9
Agreement on Agriculture (Uruguay
    Round), 118–21
agribusiness, 64
agriculture: *chakra* system, 50;
    chemical, 5, 41; colleges, 97;
    greenhouse gas production, 133;
    mechanised, 11, 15; prairie-style,
    12; productivity, 4; proportional
    aid cut, 162; sustainable, 19, 42,
    46, 64, 82, 137; Third world
    spending cuts, 160; TNC
    domination, 121; world output, 38
agroecology, 41
Algeria, 12, 138
Altieri, Miguel, 1, 29, 41

Amazon: Indians of, 83; rainforest, 87
Andean Community Irrigation
    Project, 79
Angola, 83
Animal Genetic Resources Group,
    FAO, 146
animals: diversity, 147; traction, 145–6;
    welfare, 16, 148
antibiotics, 16
Asia: cattle, 144; cereal output, 38;
    financial crisis, 36; irrigated land,
    67
Association Tefy Saina, Madagascar, 45
AstraZeneca, 124
Aswan Dam, 68
Australia, fishing quotas, 152
Austria, 17

bananas, 23, 122, 127
Bangladesh, 34, 45, 112, 164; climate
    vulnerability, 133; Grameen Bank,
    101–2; irrigation, 78; TRDEP, 102
BankCheck, 156
Barcelona, World Bank meeting
    cancellation, 157
barley, 10; winter, 57
Barnard, Thomas, 26
Baron, Sado, 69
Bayer, 62
beans, 95, 97
Beckman, David, 161
Beddington, John, 152

beekeeping, 145
beet sugar, 25
Belguim Fund for Survival, 103
Benin, cotton, 24
Benue river, 74
biodiversity, 65, 92; hotspots, 3; loss,
     5, 29, 139
'biotechnology', 27
Bishop, John, 143
Blundell, Kevin, 166
Botswana, 44, 72, 145
Bovine Spongiform Encephalopathy
     (BSE), 16–17, 148
Brazil, 6; Amazon forest, 141; cocoa,
     25; coffee, 24, 154; land reform,
     82, 84, 87; Landless Movement
     (MST), 86; Movement of Dam
     Affected People, 69; Santa
     Catarina, 49; slum dwellers, 32
Bread for the World, 161
Brecht, Bertolt, 4, 115
Britain, 11; abattoir centralisation, 16;
     agriculture, 12; farms reduction,
     15; shepherds, 18
British American Tobacco, 26
Brown, Lester, 147
buddhism, 4
Burkina Faso, 46, 72, 75, 95, 138, 164

Cambodia, 83, 88
Cameroon, 74, 97, 142; Cocoa
     Rehabilitation Project, 155
cane sugar, 25
carbon dioxide, 134
Cargill corporation, Minneapolis,
     122–3
Cariappa, Julie, 47
Cariappa Vivek, 47
Caribbean, 91, 94, 110, 158; banana
     plantations, 23
Carlier, Hans, 20
cassava, 22, 59, 94, 105, 124; varieties,
     54
Central African republic, 142
Central America, 10
centrifugal pump, 70
cereals, 116; aid, 159; milling, 96;
     output, 38
Chalmers, Camille, 164
chickens, 144–5

children, global death rate, 8
Chile, 72, 88; Biobo river dam, 155
Chimfwembe, Stephenia, 99
China, 10, 21–3, 44–5, 54, 116;
     agriculture modernisation, 17;
     beef, 147; climate vulnerability,
     133; famines, 11; farm output, 82;
     fish production, 149; grain
     demand, 148; Huang River, 135;
     meat demand, 143; rubber, 25;
     rural population decrease, 17;
     Three Gorges Dam, 155
Christian Aid, 166
Ciba–Geigy, IRRI grant, 56
Côte d'Ivoire, 53, 154; Cocoa Trade
     Project, 155
Coalition for Fair Fishing Agreements
     (CFFA), 151
cocoa, 122, 126–7; oversupply, 155;
     prices, 25
coffee, 117, 122, 126–7; 'fair trade',
     125; GM, 61; price collpase, 24,
     105, 154
Collins, Joseph, 83
Colombia: CIAT, 55; land tenure
     reform, 83–4
colonialism, 13, 115
commodity agreements, 128
Common Fund for Commodities,
     Amsterdam, 51
'Common Ground, Common Future',
     2
Commonwealth Secretariat, 127
Congo, 142
Congo, Democratic Republic of, 142
Consultative Group for International
     Agricultural Research (CGIAR),
     52, 57–60, 148
contour grass barriers, 49
Cornell Univesity, 45
cotton: GM, 60; India, 18; organic,
     24–5; pesticides, 117
Country Women Association of
     Nigeria, 102
'cover crops', 136
COWAN, Nigeria, 103
credit, 7, 87; access to, 93, 95, 100,
     102–3; facilities, 137; low-cost
     schemes, 158; micro, 106;
     questionable, 104–6

crop-drying technology, 97
crops: export, 13–14, 23–4, 51, 61, 91, 104–5, 117, 126; GM, 64–5; irrigated, 42; legume, 96, 99; narcotic, 118; 'orphan', 55; patents, 165; plantation, 122; rotation, 11–12, 135
Crucible Group, 30, 139
Cuba, 112
cultural norms, sexist, 94

dams: big, 67–70, 155–6; schemes, 6; small-scale, 70, 72
David, Lino de, 87
deep dig rejuvenation, 46
deforestation, 140–2, 156
degradation, environmental, 15
Denmark, 11
desertification, 12, 138–9
Development Organisation for People's Empowerment, 99
Diouf, Jacques, 34, 91, 160, 162
Dominican Republic, 72
drainage, 74; canals, 76
drought, 138; conditions, 37; resistance, 63; -tolerance, 43
drug abuse, 110
Du Pont, 122; patents, 124
'dumping', 15, 120
'dust bowls', 129

Earth Summit 1992 declaration, 108
'eco-agriculture', 3
economies of scale, 28
Ecuador, 6; Agricultural Service Central, 79; permaculture, 50
education, 111; fees, 7; Quicha community, 50; rights to, 114; Shipibo people, 50; women's access, 95, 98
Egypt, 67; climate vulnerability, 133
El Salvador, 154; land ownership, 82
employment, rural, 107–8
energy: dietary, 33; fossil, 130; sources, 111–12; Western agriculture use, 18
Equatorial Guinea, 142, 154–5
Ethiopia, 45, 51, 93, 138, 154, 164; cattle, 144; Cheha Integrated Rural Development Project, 45;

Coffee and Tea Authority, 51; debt burden, 39; extension workers, 38
ethylene, 61
European Union (EU), 16–17, 25, 120, 125; CAP, 15; subsidies, 14, 118
Evans, Chris, 48 export crops, 13–14, 23–4, 51, 91, 104–5; falling prices, 117, 126; taxes, 127–8
extension services/advice: access to, 93; women's access to, 93; workers, 110

falling flood agriculture, 73
famines, 131; China, 12
farmers: British incomes, 15; resource-poor/small scale, 2, 3, 100–1, 113, 123, 136, 143, 163; Third World, 13
farming, contracted, 123
farmland, conglomerised, 15, 17
Feingold, Mike, 43
female-headed households, 92, 96
fertilisers: chemical, 13, 38, 44, 136; green, 43, 46, 48–9, 51, 136; plant-based, 47
FIAN, human rights group, 86
firewood cutting, 138
Fischler, Franz, 16
fish/fishing, 8; farming, 92; fisheries, 108; overfishing, 149–50, 152; production, 50, 133; production systems, 131; Third World exports, 151
flooding: patterns, 74; plains, 73, risk, 130
fog, water collection, 72
Food First, 85
food: aid, 15; cheap imports, 12; inequality, 37; insecurity, 2, 85, 120; security, 35, 93; self-sufficiency, 123; shortages, 3, 40; trading, 115; unequal distribution, 34
foot-and-mouth disease, 16
forests, tropical, 142
France, 17; CIRAD research network, 53
fuel, 146
Future Harvest, 2

G-7, debt cancellation promises, 164
Gabon, 142
Gambia, 97
Gandhi, Mahatma, 4
Gandhi, Rajiv, 68
GATT, Agreement on Agriculture,
    118
gender bias, 94; inequalities, 98
genetic engineering, 7, 98
genetic modification (GM), 4, 6, 27,
    53, 57, 59–65
Geneva: International Trade Centre,
    51; protests, 3
German Agro Action, 86
Ghana, 59, 136; Akosombo dam, 155;
    Otuasken Rural Bank, 104
Gillet, Pierre, 151
Global Biodiversity Assessment of the
    UN Environment Programme, 30
global climate, 141; warming, 7–8, 37,
    129–3
globalisation, food chain, 16
gluten protein, 21
goats, 144
Grameen Bank, Bangladesh, 101–2
Grapes of Wrath, The, 13, 129
Greece, 11
green manures, 43, 48–9, 136
'Green Revolution', 22, 26, 28, 53,
    136, 139
greenhouse gases, 129–30, 133
Greenpeace South-east Asia, 65
Guatemala, 12; land tenure reform,
    84
Gulati, Ashok, 78

Haiti, 34, 164
Hammond, Keith, 146
hand cultivators, 96
Harvard University, 157
Hawaii, 112
healthcare, 108–9, 164
Heavily Indebted Poor Countries
    (HIPC) initiative, 163–4
Henandez, Von, 65
herbicide-resistance, 60
Herren, Hans, 65
Hinduism, 4
HIV/AIDS, 92, 103, 108–11
Honduras, International Meeting of

Landless Peasants, 86; land tenure
    reform, 84
Hook, Lars, 17
Human Development Report, 65
hunger, 2, 20, 32, 36; productivity
    losses, 33
hydroelectricity, 68
hydroponics, 134

illiteracy, 95
Imperial College, London, 152
indebtedness, 104, 163; foreign, 126
India, 21–2, 44, 72, 78, 84, 107, 164;
    cattle, 144; cotton farmers, 18;
    Council of Agricultural Research,
    55; farmers, 17; GM cotton, 60;
    Green Revolution, 28; HIV, 110;
    ICRISAT, 55; land reform, 82;
    marginal land, 139; Narmada river
    dam, 155; National Council for
    Applied Economic Research, 78;
    northwest, 71; Patents Act 1970,
    124; Pondicherry, 47; rice, 7, 26,
    30, 116, 140; rubber, 25; That
    desert, 144; Uttar Pradesh, 70
Indonesia, 22, 45, 154; climate
    vulnerability, 133; cocoa, 25; forest
    plantation, 141; land tenure
    reform, 84; poverty increase, 36
Industrial Revolution, 11
inequality, inefficiencies of, 83
inputs: costs, 29–30, 56; price increase,
    120
Integrated Coffee Technologies Inc.,
    61
intellectual property rights, 62–3, 124
intercropping, 5, 26–7, 51
interest, rates of, 104
Intergovernmental Panel on Climate
    Change, 8
Intermediate Technology Group, 18
International Agricultural Research
    Centres (IARCs), 52–3, 55–8
International Centre for Agricultural
    Research in Dry Areas, Syria
    (ICARDA), 55, 58
International Centre for Tropical
    Agriculture, Colombia, 54–5, 58
International Centre of Insect
    Physiology and Ecology, 65

International Collective in Support of Fishworkers, 151
International Crops Research Institute for the Semi-Arid Tropics (ICRISAT), India, 55
International Food Policy Research Institute, Washington, 59, 148
International Fund for Agricultural Development (IFAD), 79, 88, 95, 158
International Institute of Tropical Agriculture, Nigeria, 55, 58
International Maize and Wheat Improvement Centre, 55
International Monetary Fund (IMF), 7, 75, 114, 117, 119, 141, 154, 156, 163; austerity conditions, 164
International Rice Research Institute, Manila (IRRI), 56–8, 62–3
International Rivers Network, California, 69
International Trade Centre, Geneva, 51
International Water Management Institute, 77, 80
internet, the, 2
Ireland, famine 1840s, 12, 116, 140
irrigation, 6, 10, 22, 42, 67–8, 70–2, 76, 78, 80, 88; Andean projects, 79; indigenous systems, 73–4, 76; Pakistan, 75; small-scale, 69
Islam, Ramadan, 4
Israel, 71

Jajarkot Permaculture Programme, Nepal, 48–9
Japan, 17; logging companies, 141
Jordan, 71; diminishing rainfall, 131–2; water re-use, 77
Jubilee 2000 campaign, 164

Kandiah, Arumugam, 76
Kaulab, Rashid, 119
Kenya, 70, 95, 154; food insecurity, 120; Laikipia project, 72; tobacco, 25
knowledge, application, 30; farming, 29
Koestler, Arthur, 166
Kramer, Marleen, 99

Kyoto Protocol of the Convention on Climate Change, 133

Lagdo Dam, 74
land: degradation, 14, 75, 131, 137–8; equitable rights to, 82; ownership concentration, 88; privatisation, 85–6; reform, 83–4; scarcity, 126; tenure, 81, 139; women ownership, 96; women's access to, 110
landlessness, 81, 87
landmines, 83
Lappe, Frances Moore, 83
Latin America, 94; potatoes, 23; rural economy, 108; unequal land system, 84
Laudanié, Henri de, 45
'layer composting', 46
learning capacity, hunger loss, 33
Libya, 12
'life sciences industry', 98
Lipton, Michael, 38
livestock, 8, 10–11, 42, 92, 131, 144–6; 'battery-cage' systems, 143; grain-fattened, 147–8; technologies, 54

Madagascar: Renitelo cattle, 147; rice, 6, 44–5, 57, 121
Mader, Harsh, 164
Madras, water supplies, 139
Mae-Wan Ho, 60
Mahadin, Mahmood, 132
maize, 10, 21–2, 72, 92, 95, 97, 124–5; blight, 140; hybrid, 106; Irish famine export, 12
Majot, Juliette, 156
Malawi, 23
Malaysia, 132; rubber, 25
Mali, 75, 105
malnutrition, HIV/AIDS, 109
Manantali Dam, 74
manure, 43, 46, 144; organic, 26
marginal environments, 27, 30, 108, 138
markets, access, 112
Mauritania, 74–5, 138
Mauritius, 112
Mayan civilization, 12
Mbugua, John, 71

McCully, Patrick, 69
McRobie, George, 18
meat, increased demand, 148
Meltzer, Allan, 157
Mexico, 44, 154; beef producers, 17;
    land tenure reform, 84; waste-
    water use, 77
microfinance institutions, 100–1, 106
millet, 10, 73, 75, 105, 124; pearl, 23,
    55; yields, 46
Mississippi River, 11
Mollison, Bill, 43
Mongolia, 34
monoculture/cropping, 5, 12–14, 26,
    28, 123, 136, 139; pests, 29;
    subsidies, 16; yield realities, 41
monopoly control, GM, 63
Monsanto, 62–3, 122; IRRI grant, 56
Morocco, 138
Mozambique, 23; floods, 133
Mucuna, 136
mulberry, 43
mulches, green, 46, 51
Murphy, Sophia, 122
Mwansa, Emma, 99

Namibia, 23; land tenure reform, 84
Nansubuga, Anna, 103–4
neo-liberalism, 86
Nepal, 23, 44, 47–8, 72; permaculture,
    6
Netherlands Development and
    Cooperation Service, 79
New Zealand, fishing quotas, 152
Nicaragua, 112, 154
Niger, 63, 70, 75; Inland Delta, 73
Nigeria, 74, 102–3, 164; cassava, 54;
    cattle, 144; COWAN, 103; IITA,
    55; Sokoto Basin, 75
North Atlantic Free Trade Agreement
    (NAFTA), 17
North Korea, 34
Novartis, 64, 124

O'Riordan, Brian, 152
oil, 24
oilseed, traders, 122
olive oil, world price, 132
organic agriculture, 16–17, 41, 43, 47,
    82; fertilisers, 136

Organisation of Petroleum Exporting
    Countries, (OPEC), 158
orphans, 110
Orynova, 62
overgrazing, 135
Oxfam, 46

Pakistan, 23, 84; waste-water use, 77
Palestine, 1, 71
palm oil, 142
patents, 121; life forms, 124; seeds,
    123
Permacultura America Latina, 50
permaculture, 6, 11, 43–4, 48–9, 50
Peru, 72
pests: biological control, 26; pesticides,
    60; monocropping prevalence, 29
Philippines, 86, 112, 120; agrarian
    reform conference, 85;
    Comprehensive Agrarian Law
    Reform, 89; forest chopping, 141;
    IRRI, 56–8, 62–3; land tenure
    reform, 83–4; Partnership for the
    Development of Human
    Resources in Rural Areas, 89; rice
    blight, 140; Rice Research
    Institute, 56
photovoltaics, 112
pigeonpea, 55
Pioneer Hi-Bred, 124
Plan of Action for Women in
    Development, FAO, 95
ploughing, 145–6
population growth, 14
post-harvesting technology, 97
potatoes, 10, 23, 95, 124–5; blight, 12,
    140
poverty, 4, 32–3, 40, 81–2, 98, 101,
    116, 161; alleviation programme,
    49; estimates, 70; 'magic bullet'
    solution, 162; reduction, 53–4;
    smallholder, 155
Prague, protest, 3
Pretty, Jules, 30
privatisation, 24, 108; agricultural
    research, 38; communal lands, 85–6
productivity: large landholdings, 82;
    per hectare, 27
Project Agro-Forestier (PAF), 46
prostitution, 110

protectionism, devices, 120
pulses, 53

Rafaralahy, Sebastién, 45
rainfall, 73
Ramirez, Marlene, 90
'recycling', 43
regenerative technologies, 42
Reunion, 112
Rhodes, Cecil, 13
rice/paddy, 6, 21–2, 26, 28, 45, 48, 73,
    75, 87, 92, 123–5; climate change
    vulnerability, 132; flooded, 76;
    Golden, 62–3; high-yield, 53;
    India, 7, 116; Madagascar, 6, 44–5,
    57, 121; Sahel region, 76; Tungro
    virus, 140; varieties, 30, 56
roads, improvement programmes, 113
Rockefeller Foundation, 62–3
Roman Empire, 12
Rome Declaration on World Food
    Security and Plan of Action, 34–6
roots, food, 42
rubber, price trend, 25
run-off techniques, 72
rural development, 107–13

Sachs, Jeffrey, 157
Salameh, Elias, 76
Saskawa Global 2000 project, 28
Schlosser, Eric, 165
Schroeder, Gerhard, 16
sea-level rises, 133
Seattle, protest, 3
seeds, 1, 63; 'banks', Andes, 92;
    business concentration, 15; edible,
    11, 17; germination, 59; global
    market, 122; ownership
    concentration, 121; patents, 123;
    selection, 26
'Seeds of Change', USA, 29
Senegal, 73–5
sewage, 77
shading, 27
Shamana, Shashore, 39
Shapiro, Howard, 29
Shell, IRRI grant, 56
'shelterbelts', 139
Shiva, Vandana, 27, 29, 98
Sikh religion, 4

slave labour, 13
small-scale fishermen, 150, 152
soil: degradation, 134–5; erosion, 12;
    fertility, 136, 138; salinity creation,
    75–6
solar energy, 112; systems, 111
Somalia, 83
sorghum, 46, 124
South Africa, 72, 86; land tenure
    reform, 84
South America, 10; tropical, 44
South Centre, 119
South Korea, 116
soybeans, 64, 124–5
staple food crops, women, 91
State of Food Insecurity in the World,
    59
state, regulation, 85
statistics, small-scale farming, 20–1
Steinbeck, John, 12, 129
Stiles, John, 61
structural adjustment policy/
    programmes, 7, 24, 75, 114, 117,
    119, 141, 163
Stum, Herve Le, 121
subsidies, 15–16; export, 119; USA,
    14; western agriculture, 120
Sudan, 71, 164; zone, 23
sugar, 117, 122, 126–7; ACP group,
    25; bagasse, 112
suicide, small-scale farmers, 18
supermarkets, 15
'superweeds', 60
swales, 50
Swaminathan, M.S., 7, 40
Sweden: Farmers Association, 17;
    organic farming, 16
sweet potatoes, 54
Switzerland, 17
Syngenta, 62, 122, 124
Syria, 1; ICARDA, 55, 58
System of Rice Intensification (SRI),
    45

Tanzania, 109, 135, 145
Tarabey, Anis, 132
tariff barriers, 14, 119; escalation, 120;
    food, 118
tea, 122, 126–7
Tennessee Valley Dam, 67

Terminator technology, 59, 63
termite activity, 46
terrorism, war on, 8
Tewolde, Egziabher Gebre, 6, 60–1
Thailand, 120; land tenure reform, 84; organic agriculture, 82; Pak Mun dam, 155; rubber, 25; sustainable rural development, 49
Threepenny Opera, 4
Tiga Dam, 74
Tinning, Gavin, 50
tobacco, 25; contracted smallholders, 26, 123
trade: concentration, 122; domination, 118; international, 116; liberalisation, 120–2, 126
Trade-Related Intellectual Property Rights (TRIPS), 124, 165
trans-national corporations (TNCs), 121, 125; expansion, 123
treadle pumps, 70–1
trees, 136; integration, 43, 48; logging, 141; olive, 132; water catching, 72
Trickle Up, 106
Trust Fund for Food Security, 40, 162
Tungro virus, 140
Turkey, 1, 21; Ilisu dam, 155
Twain, Mark, 81

Uganda, 92, 154; Bujagli dam, 155; Women's Efforts to Save Orphans, 103
unemployment, 28, 36; rural, 33
Union Carbide, IRRI grant, 56
United Nations (UN): Conference on Trade and Development Report, 125; Commission on Genetic Resources, 64; Convention to Combat Desertification, 139; Development Programme, 53, 65, 99, 145, 156; Environment Programme, 30; Food and Agriculture Organisation (FAO), 6, 20, 28, 34, 36–8, 40, 53, 59, 67, 70, 76, 93, 95, 99, 108–13, 117, 131, 134–6, 138, 140, 143, 146, 149, 156–7, 161–3; Intergovernmental Panel on Climate Change, 133, 133; International Fund for Agricultural

Development, 105, 114, 132; World Food Programme, 158–9
United States of America (USA), 12, 15, 17, 67, 120, 124; Congressional International Financial Instiution Committee, 156; food consumption, 147; Institute for Agriculture and Trade Policy, 122; Kyoto refusal, 133; maize blight, 140; 'Seeds of Change', 29; soya exports, 17;
subsidies, 14, 118
University of Essex, database, 42
University of Hawaii, 61
University of Jordan, 76
University of Sussex
University of Wisconsin, 64
'Unumli-Arpa', winter barley, 57
Uruguay Round, GATT, 118

Vavilov, Nikolai, 57
vegetables, 10, 92, 97, 116
Via Campesina, 85–6
Vietnam, 44, 164; coffee, 105, 154; farmers, 104
Vitamin A deficiency (VAD), 62–3

Washington, protest, 3
water, 6, 38; availability, 66; clean, 39; erosion, 135; harvesting techniques, 71–2; infiltration, 46; Madras supplies, 139; management, 75; pollution, 18; pricing, 79; re-cycling, 76–7; rights, 80; scarcity, 67; stress, 130; table, 78; wells, 73, 78
water-wheel pump, Uttar Pradesh, 70
Watson, Robert T., 130
weeds, 27, 136; 'super', 60; weeding, 96
West Africa, 17, 73; cocoa, 25
wet-season flooding, 75
wheat, 10, 28, 92, 124–5, 132, 140; Durum, 21; high-yield, 53; modified, 55; yields, 132
widows, 110
wildlife, 3
wind erosion, 135
Wintock International, 28
women: AIDS vulnerability, 110;

credit access, 103; farmers, 54, 91–9; groups, 72; land, 84

Women in Agriculture Conference 1998, 98

World Bank, 2–3, 7, 8, 18, 28, 53, 69, 75, 79, 84–6, 95, 101, 104, 114, 117, 119, 141, 153–5, 163–4; Barcelona cancellation, 157; Operational Directive on Poverty Reduction, 87; Prague protests, 157; Tropical Forestry Action Plan, 156

World Commission on Dams, 68, 156

World Conservation Union, 2

World Food Conference 1974, 158

World Food Summit 1996, 2, 34, 36–7, 161–6

World Food Summit+5, 39–40, 157

World Health Organisation, 62

World Overview of Conservation Approaches and Technologies (WOCAT), 137

World Resources Institute, Washington, 156

World Trade Centre atrocity, 8–9

World Trade Organisation, 117–20, 124, 165

Worldwatch Institute, 147

Younissi, Saley, 63

Yunus, Mohammed, 101

Zai holes, 46

Zambia, 7, 23, 70, 96, 98, 105, 114, 145, 154; pumps, 71

Zeneca Mogen, 62

Zimbabwe, 23, 44, 70; land reform, 83–4; maize varieties, 140; pumps, 71

The Global Issues Series

Already available

Robert Ali Brac de la Perrière and Franck Seuret, *Brave New Seeds: The Threat of GM Crops to Farmers*

Oswaldo de Rivero, *The Myth of Development: The Non-viable Economies of the 21st Century*

Joyeeta Gupta, *Our Simmering Planet: What to do about Global Warming?*

Nicholas Guyatt, *Another American Century? The United States and the World after 2000*

Martin Khor, *Rethinking Globalization: Critical Issues and Policy Choices*

John Madeley, *Food for All: The Need for a New Agriculture*

John Madeley, *Hungry for Trade: How the Poor Pay for Free Trade*

Riccardo Petrella, *The Water Manifesto: Arguments for a World Water Contract*

Vandana Shiva, *Protect or Plunder? Understanding Intellectual Property Rights*

Harry Shutt, *A New Democracy: Alternatives to a Bankrupt World Order*

David Sogge, *Give and Take: What's the Matter with Foreign Aid?*

In preparation

Peggy Antrobus and Gigi Francisco, *The Women's Movement Worldwide: Issues and Strategies for the New Century*

Amit Bhaduri and Deepak Nayyar, *Free Market Economics: The Intelligent Person's Guide to Liberalization*

Jonathan Bloch and Paul Todd, *Business as Usual? Intelligence Agencies and Secret Services in the New Century*

Julian Burger, *First Peoples: What Future?*

Richard Douthwaite, *Go for Growth? Poverty, the Environment and the Pros and Cons of Economic Growth*

Graham Dunkley, *Trading Development: Trade, Globalization and Alternative Development Possibilities*

Ha-Joon Chang and Ilene Grabel, *There is No Alternative? Myths and Realities about Development Policy Alternatives*

John Howe, *A Ticket to Ride: Breaking the Transport Gridlock*

Calestous Juma, *The New Genetic Divide: Biotechnology in the Age of Globalization*

Roger Moody, *Digging the Dirt: the Modern World of Global Mining*

Jeremy Seabrook, *The Future of Culture: Can Human Diversity Survive in a Globalized World?*

Keith Suter, *Curbing Corporate Power: How Can We Control Transnational Corporations?*

Nedd Willard, *The Drugs War: Is This the Solution?*

For full details of this list and Zed's other subject and general catalogues, please write to: The Marketing Department, Zed Books, 7 Cynthia Street, London NI 9JF, UK or email Sales@zedbooks. demon.co.uk
Visit our website at: www.zedbooks.demon.co.uk

PARTICIPATING ORGANIZATIONS

Both ENDS A service and advocacy organization which collaborates with environment and indigenous organizations, both in the South and in the North, with the aim of helping to create and sustain a vigilant and effective environmental movement.

> Damrak 28-30, 1012 LJ Amsterdam, The Netherlands
> Phone: +31 20 623 0823   Fax: +31 20 620 8049
> Email: info@bothends.org
> Website: www.bothends.org

Catholic Institute for International Relations (CIIR) CIIR aims to contribute to the eradication of poverty through a programme that combines advocacy at national and international level with community-based development.

> Unit 3, Canonbury Yard, 190a New North Road, London N1 7BJ, UK
> Phone +44 (0)20 7354 0883   Fax +44 (0)20 7359 0017
> Email: ciir@ciir.org
> Website: www.ciir.org

Corner House The Corner House is a UK-based research and solidarity group working on social and environmental justice issues in North and South.

> PO Box 3137, Station Road, Sturminster Newton, Dorset DT10 1YJ, UK
> Tel.: +44 (0)1258 473795   Fax: +44 (0)1258 473748
> Email: cornerhouse@gn.apc.org
> Website: www.cornerhouse.icaap.org

Council on International and Public Affairs (CIPA) CIPA is a human rights research, education and advocacy group, with a particular focus on economic and social rights in the USA and elsewhere around the world. Emphasis in recent years has been given to resistance to corporate domination.

> 777 United Nations Plaza, Suite 3C, New York, NY 10017, USA
> Tel. +1 212 972 9877   Fax +1 212 972 9878
> E-mail: cipany@igc.org
> Website: www.cipa-apex.org

Dag Hammarskjöld Foundation The Dag Hammarskjöld Foundation, established 1962, organises seminars and workshops on social, economic and cultural issues facing developing countries with a particular focus on alternative and innovative solutions. Results are published in its journal *Develpment Dialogue*.

Övre Slottsgatan 2, 753 10 Uppsala, Sweden.
Tel.: +46 18 102772   Fax: +46 18 122072
e-mail: secretariat@dhf.uu.se
Website: www.dhf.uu.se

Development GAP   The Development Group for Alternative Policies
is a Non-Profit Development Resource Organization working with
popular organizations in the South and their Northern partners in support of a development that is truly sustainable and that advances social
justice.

927 15th Street NW, 4th Floor, Washington, DC, 20005, USA
Tel.: +1 202 898 1566   Fax: +1 202 898 1612
E-mail: dgap@igc.org
Website: www.developmentgap.org

Focus on the Global South   Focus is dedicated to regional and
global policy analysis and advocacy work. It works to strengthen the
capacity of organizations of the poor and marginalized people of the
South and to better analyse and understand the impacts of the globalization process on their daily lives.

C/o CUSRI, Chulalongkorn University, Bangkok 10330, Thailand
Tel.: +66 2 218 7363 Fax: +66 2 255 9976
Email: Admin@focusweb.org
Website: www.focusweb.org

Inter Pares   Inter Pares, a Canadian social justice organization, has
been active since 1975 in building relationships with Third World
development groups and providing support for community-based
development programs. Inter Pares is also involved in education and
advocacy in Canada, promoting understanding about the causes, effects
and solutions to poverty.

58 rue Arthur Street, Ottawa, Ontario, KIR 7B9 Canada
Phone +1 613 563 4801   Fax +1 613 594 4704

Public Interest Research Centre   PIRC is a research and campaign-
ing group based in Delhi which seeks to serve the information needs of
activists and organizations working on macro-economic issues concerning finance, trade and development.

142 Maitri Apartments, Plot No. 28, Patparganj, Delhi 110092, India
Phone: +91 11 2221081/2432054   Fax: +91 11 2224233
Email: kaval@nde.vsnl.net.in

Third World Network TWN is an international network of groups and individuals involved in efforts to bring about a greater articulation of the needs and rights of peoples in the Third World; a fair distribution of the world's resources; and forms of development which are ecologically sustainable and fulfil human needs. Its international secretariat is based in Penang, Malaysia.

228 Macalister Road, 10400 Penang, Malaysia
Tel.: +60 4 226 6159   Fax: +60 4 226 4505
Email: twnet@po.jaring.my
Website: www.twnside.org.sg

Third World Network–Africa TWN–Africa is engaged in research and advocacy on economic, environmental and gender issues. In relation to its current particular interest in globalization and Africa, its work focuses on trade and investment, the extractive sectors and gender and economic reform.

2 Ollenu Street, East Legon, PO Box AN19452, Accra-North, Ghana.
Tel.: +233 21 511189/503669/500419   Fax: +233 21 511188
email: twnafrica@ghana.com

World Development Movement (WDM) The World Development Movement campaigns to tackle the causes of poverty and injustice. It is a democratic membership movement that works with partners in the South to cancel unpayable debt and break the ties of IMF conditionality, for fairer trade and investment rules, and for strong international rules on multinationals.

25 Beehive Place, London SW9 7QR, UK
Tel.: +44 (0)20 7737 6215   Fax: +44 (0)20 7274 8232
E-mail: wdm@wdm.org.uk
Website: www.wdm.org.uk

THIS BOOK IS ALSO AVAILABLE
IN THE FOLLOWING COUNTRIES

EGYPT

MERIC
(The Middle East Readers'
Information Center)
2 Bahgat Ali Street,
Tower D/Apt. 24
Zamalek
Cairo
Tel: 20 2 735 3818/736 3824
Fax: 20 2 736 9355

FIJI

University Book Centre,
University of South Pacific,
Suva
Tel: 679 313 900
Fax: 679 303 265

GHANA

EPP Book Services,
PO Box TF 490,
Trade Fair,
Accra
Tel: 233 21 778347
Fax: 233 21 779099

MOZAMBIQUE

Sul Sensações
PO Box 2242,
Maputo
Tel: 258 1 421974
Fax: 258 1 423414

NAMIBIA

Book Den
PO Box 3469
Shop 4, Frans Indongo Gardens
Windhoek
Tel: 264 61 239976
Fax: 264 61 234248

NEPAL

Everest Media Services,
GPO Box 5443, Dillibazar
Putalisadak Chowk

Kathmandu
Tel: 977 1 416026
Fax: 977 1 250176

PAPUA NEW GUINEA

Unisearch PNG Pty Ltd
Box 320, University
National Capital District
Tel: 675 326 0130
Fax: 675 326 0127

RWANDA

Librairie Ikirezi
PO Box 443
Kigali
Tel/Fax: 250 71314

SUDAN

The Nile Bookshop
New Extension Street 41
P O Box 8036
Khartoum
Tel: 249 11 463749

TANZANIA

TEMA Publishing Co Ltd
PO Box 63115
Dar Es Salaam
Tel: 255 22 2113608
Fax: 255 22 2110472

UGANDA

Aristoc Booklex Ltd
PO Box 5130, Kampala Road
Diamond Trust Building
Kampala
Tel: 256 41 344381/349052
Fax: 256 41 254867

ZAMBIA

UNZA Press
PO Box 32379
Lusaka
Tel: 260 1 290409
Fax: 260 1 253952